THE
FLY CREEK CIDER MILL
COOKBOOK

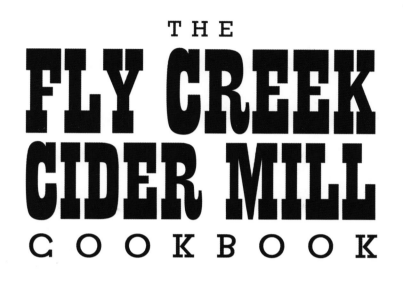

THE
FLY CREEK
CIDER MILL
COOKBOOK

MORE THAN 100
DELICIOUS
APPLE RECIPES

BRENDA AND BILL MICHAELS

SURREY BOOKS

AN AGATE IMPRINT

CHICAGO

Printed in China.

Food photography copyright © 2016 Steve Poole.

Library of Congress Cataloging-in-Publication Data

Names: Michaels, Brenda, author. | Michaels, Bill (Howard William), author.
Title: The Fly Creek Cider Mill cookbook : more than 100 delicious apple
 recipes / by Brenda and Bill Michaels.
Description: Chicago : Surrey Books, an Agate Imprint, [2016]
Identifiers: LCCN 2015050521 (print) | LCCN 2016006697 (ebook) | ISBN
 9781572841949 (pbk.) | ISBN 157284194X (pbk.) | ISBN 9781572847781 (ebook)
 | ISBN 1572847786 (ebook)
Subjects: LCSH: Cooking (Apples) | Fly Creek Cider Mill (Fly Creek, N.Y.) |
 LCGFT: Cookbooks.
Classification: LCC TX813.A6 .M564 2016 (print) | LCC TX813.A6 (ebook) | DDC
 641.6/411--dc23
LC record available at http://lccn.loc.gov/2015050521

10 9 8 7 6 5 4 3 2 1   16 17 18 19 20

Surrey is an imprint of Agate Publishing. Agate books are available in bulk at discount prices.

agatepublishing.com

For our wonderful children, Sadie and Henry Michaels, who have grown up in a very hectic business and learned to be helpful, friendly, and kind to everyone they meet.

Contents

Drinks 184

A Brief History of the Fly Creek Cider Mill and Orchard

IF NORMAN ROCKWELL were alive today, he could visit the Fly Creek Cider Mill in the spring at the edge of Fly Creek in New York and paint an image that would easily provoke thoughts of an earlier time in America: the gentle flow of the creek waters, the flowering apple trees, the pond overflowing with ducks and geese with their newly hatched chicks toodling right behind them, the bustle of Mill employees setting up for the upcoming season, and our whole family bursting with pride at the success of this old-time family-owned business. And, the picture created would, for sure, bring smiles and sentimental longing just as most of his other paintings do.

Even though we work there every day, to us the Fly Creek Cider Mill holds the essence of another era. It has a long history beginning in the mid-1800s when Hosea Williams built a centralized

HOSEA WILLIAMS'S CIDER MILL AT FLYCREEK.

1897 newspaper coverage of the Fly Creek Cider Mill.

cider mill to more efficiently turn apples into cider. Because they had been grown from seed rather than root stock (and we can blame Johnny Appleseed for that), most of the apples found throughout the eastern part of the United States were sour. This suited early settlers just fine as their main use was in the preparation of hard cider and applejack, the meal-time beverages of choice. For the most part, all cider was homemade, hand pressed, and time consuming to make. When Hosea opened his mill, he used a turbine and the creek waters to run a state-of-the-art Boomer & Boschert water-hydraulic press and grinder to rapidly process fruit to drink. As you can imagine, all of the farmers and locals quickly turned away from their labor-intensive hand presses and brought their apples to the Mill for processing.

While waiting for their apples to be turned into cider, the community watched the fascinating, new-fangled machinery work as they picnicked and gossiped with neighbors. Every bushel of apples produced 3 gallons of cider, so creating a goodly supply of beverage to last the winter months while taking a couple of hours of relaxation was more than appreciated. Once back home, the cider—usually in a barrel—was lowered into a root cellar and sweetened. Each family had a closely held secret for turning sweet cider into hard—a secret that was usually only passed down to family members. Don't we wish we had some of those secrets today?

Through the end of the 1800s, the Mill flourished as Hosea Williams expanded its services to meet the needs of a growing population. Once apple pressing was over, the turbine was used to power a wood lathe, jigsaw, and planer to fashion the fancy wood-work that would decorate many of the large, ornate houses being built in Fly Creek and nearby Cooperstown (where many of those houses still stand, showcasing this early woodwork). Shavings from the woodworking served as insulation for the blocks of ice cut from the frozen pond in the winter months, which could then be sold throughout the year. A grist mill was added to grind corn and wheat. Innovation continued with the introduction of each new addition, and the Mill became a focal point of many community activities.

By the turn of the 19th century, the Mill had been purchased by Linn Kane, who introduced a Waterloo Boy—a two-cylinder gas engine—to run the grinder. This lowered the dependence upon the creek waters during the drier months, so the enterprise could run at capacity all year long. Unfortunately, as the century moved on, the temperance brigades took charge and the production of hard cider was banished, particularly in rural areas. By 1920 the entire country was dry, and no cider was produced at all during Prohibition. By the end of this dry period, beer consumption had risen and the large-scale production of beer was done far more inexpensively than cider. At this point, almost no cider production survived. Somehow the Fly Creek Cider Mill remained in business by doing small-lot custom pressing and woodworking until the 1950s when Linn closed it. Referred to as the "old mill," no one thought that it would ever become a vital part of the community again.

The run-down Mill seemed to be part of the almost forgotten past, but in 1962 a newly married couple of young locals, Bill's parents, Barbara and Charlie Michaels, looked at the Mill property as their future. It was the miller's residence on the street corner of the plot that they fancied as a home for their hoped-for family. They had no interest in the dormant Mill. However, Linn Kane, seeing the expectancy in the young couple's eyes, sold them the property at a very low price without letting them know that it was done in the hope that they would breathe new life into the Mill itself.

The task of restoring the house was huge, but Charlie, a skilled craftsman, was up to the job. Barbara, a grade school art teacher, used her creativity and artistry to turn Charlie's work into an efficient and beautifully decorated home. With a watchful eye, Linn had a feeling that the Mill might be their next renovation project, so he regaled them with stories of the golden years when wagons lined the street to the corner, waiting for apple pressing to begin. The stories took hold, and the couple fell hook, line, and sinker.

Watercolor portrait of present-day founders Barbara and Charlie Michaels.

Delighted with the potential of starting a family business in their own backyard, Charlie and Barbara relished the job of shoring up the structure and cleaning the years of neglect from the pressing area. Cider work started off very slowly, as they still had jobs and Bill and his older sister, Francine, to care for. Friends pitched in, and the revitalization turned into fun. Early on, Charlie planted the first orchard and, during the fall season, friends helped truck apples from afar to meet the needs of the weekend pressings. Customers from the olden days brought their own apples in, and Charlie was delighted to do custom pressing, just like the old times of Hosea Williams and Linn Kane. He learned the quirks of the water press and grew to love his time working with it. Bill, even when very young, was his assistant and took to pressing just like the ducklings on the pond took to water. Barrels were filled and fermented; the Mill was quickly on track to become a thriving business.

Although the business of cider making was primary, Barbara began selling her art wares and the work of local craftspeople in her own Olde Mill Shoppe on the second floor of the pressing build-

From left to right: Filling customer jugs from the original tank; Charlie's first of many additions to the Mill, circa 1971; Lesner turbines first removal for restoration. Bill, Charlie, and Francine Michaels.

ing in place of the original grist mill. Homemade cider doughnuts (see page 39), apple bread, and molasses crinkle cookies (see page 181) found a place right beside Barbara's traditional dried flower arrangements. With the addition of local maple syrup and honey, a true farm-to-table and store business was begun long before it was the "in" thing to do. Retail sales grew and rather than running a "hobby" business a few weekends in the fall, Charlie and Barbara realized that with a little more effort, investment, and marketing skill, the "hobby" could become a full-time business, and that is just what they went about doing.

Expansion began with an enlarged sales room and a more diverse product mix, but the focus stayed on local upstate products. The marketing plan positioned the Fly Creek Cider Mill as a fall family attraction where "tradition is kept alive." After many busy years with Francine helping in the store and Bill helping with the pressing, the Mill was once again a thriving part of the Fly Creek community. Visitors to the National Baseball Hall of Fame in Cooperstown made it an equally important destination, and locals appreciated the unique entertainment and shopping the Mill brought to their community. Fall once again meant extraordinary cider and fun-filled days feeding the ducks, watching the ancient— but still functioning—water press pour out fresh, aromatic apple cider, and indulging in local foods and crafts. And, for Barbara and Charlie, the idea that a small, family-run business had thrived made their work even more rewarding.

"For Barbara and Charlie, the idea that a small, family-run business had thrived made their work even more rewarding."

As Bill's parents began thinking about retirement, we were newly married. Thinking ahead to raising a family, we were looking for something to do that would keep us in the bucolic area of our childhood. Bill had worked during the fall at the Mill his entire life, and although he had built a career in the hospitality industry, he always loved coming back "home." Brenda, trained as a graphic designer and interior architect, had ventured far from home but always returned to the quiet rural setting. Together, we felt that the Mill might be just the thing for us. With Charlie and Barbara's blessing, we purchased the Mill from them and set out to build another generation of Mill innovation.

We immediately expanded the Mill's traditional fall season to include all of the summer months. This was followed by the addition of a broader range of products and hard-to-find specialty foods as well as an in-demand classic New York State Mill-aged Cheddar cheese. To accommodate the overflow of crowds, restrooms were

Bill Michaels learning the retail trade from his grandfather (Hi Michaels) at the family's market on historic Main Street in Cooperstown, established in 1873.

Newspaper coverage of Charlie and Barbara's first year at the Mill.

added along with a rustic stairway to the upper-floor selling room as well as a platform for watching the cider pressing. A cold-storage room was converted into a pack-your-own apple display room where visitors could make their own selection of fresh-from-the-orchard apples. The small orchard at the Mill couldn't supply the amount of apples needed for the thousands of gallons of cider pressed annually, so the Mill began purchasing apples from farmers throughout the area, thus helping to keep local orchards in continual production.

Today, we keep the Mill open for most of the year, as it has become a must-visit destination for tourists to the Cooperstown/ Leatherstocking area. It is seen as a mecca of agritourism for people wanting to experience the flavors of Central New York through farm-direct, Pride of New York products such as apple salsas and butters, apple cider doughnuts, apple pies and breads, maple syrup, and, of course, our famous sweet cider. We are big supporters of the Pride of New York program as it is the State's branding program for the promotion of agricultural products grown, produced, or processed in New York State. The program markets those of us who participate and informs consumers about the availability and variety of New York–produced or –processed products.

Continuing the innovative thrust of our parents while considering the Mill's heritage, we have become a New York Farm Winery, producing hard ciders and apple wines, which are sampled next to many other New York varietal wines in the store. The Mill's storefront restaurant offers wines and hard cider by the glass, cider floats (see page 185), cider slushies (see page 186),

and cold, refreshing glasses of sweet cider along with sandwiches and other treats.

Just like the early days when the Mill was the gathering place for local families, fall weekends find thousands of people watching the now 20,000 gallons of cider produced by the Mill's original water-powered press. During other times of the year, visitors can view the process through video in the Cider Gallery exhibit. The Mill pond continues to be a gathering place for both visitors and wildlife; a boardwalk allows visitors to view and feed the birds, as the pond hosts several breeds of ducks and geese that anxiously squawk for corn. Chickens roost in a hut and give children a chance to see where eggs come from.

Whether it is through educational exhibits, new products, traditional entertainment, and farm activities, or just adapting flavors of the past to the present, we—along with our children, Sadie and Henry—have invested our hope in a future of diversification and innovation. As the Fly Creek Cider Mill moves into its 160th year, we are ready to welcome new generations to the experience of life down by the old millstream.

—Brenda and Bill Michaels

From left to right: "Broom people," created by Barbara, are displayed in the fall; seasonal floral displays welcome visitors; one of many tasty treats at the snack barn and bakery.

About
Cider and
Apples

BEFORE APPLE TREES were planted in the early colonies, home-brewed, low-alcohol beers were the drink of choice in part because plain water had not been considered a drinkable beverage in the old country. This was probably a good thing because fresh water was often bacteria laden and the cause of a quick and painful death. Once apple trees were planted from seeds sent from England, cider making followed shortly thereafter. Being mildly alcoholic, cider inhibited bacteria growth, was easy to store, and safe to drink. Even children drank a version called ciderkin, a weak mix created by soaking pomace (the solid remains comprised of the apple skin, seeds, and pulp left after pressing the juice out) in boiled water.

By the beginning of the 1800s, cider was a major commodity throughout New England. In fact, at that time it is said that the average resident of the Massachusetts colony drank 35 gallons of cider annually. It was also around this time that John Chapman, better known as Johnny Appleseed, began his trip westward

proselytizing for his church and cultivating small apple orchards all along the way. Through his work, homesteaders and pioneers heading further west had cider to drink and saplings to transplant in new territories.

Cider remained America's most popular drink until the early 1900s when an influx of Eastern European and German immigrants introduced their love of beers and ales to their new neighbors. Since cultivating grains and barley was more in tune with the soil of the heartland, brewing supplanted cider pressing and cider drinking slowly passed from favor. Then, the advent of the Volstead Act and its prohibition of alcoholic beverages was the nail in the coffin. Not only did the Act prohibit the sale of hard cider, it limited the amount of sweet cider produced to 200 gallons per orchard. On top of this, the volatile prohibitionist movement sent members out to burn cider orchards to the ground, leaving none of the necessary tart, cider-making apples to survive. For all intents, cider making died with Prohibition.

It took almost another century for interest in cider making to return. Of course, there were a few small mills, like the Fly Creek Cider Mill, that pressed fresh cider in the fall, but they were few and far between. Throughout these years, apple production grew dramatically, but the orchards were focused on sweet eating and cooking apples, not the tart, heirloom apples needed to make great cider. As the farm-to-table movement has grown and as more young farmers turn to artisanal products to keep their farms and orchards alive, cider pressing and drinking has returned.

Making Cider

Because in the early years of American cider production the apples used were seed-grown and very sour, cider was very, very low in alcohol. This was because the apples were so low in the sugar necessary to feed the yeasts in the juice. When making cider, the yeasts quickly eat what little sugar the juice contains, turning it into alcohol and carbon dioxide. Once the sugar has been consumed, there is no more to replenish it and the yeasts die, leaving a very slightly fermented drink.

At the Fly Creek Cider Mill, the production area is on the second level in the Cider Gallery. The Gallery overlooks the original cider-making equipment that the Mill still uses. Pressing occurs only at nonscheduled times, except during the fall when the machinery runs continuously from 10 a.m. until 2 p.m. every weekend. At other times a video demonstrates the cider-making process. Because Bill has been involved in cider pressing since he was little, he remains the overseer and the main mechanic in fixing and repairing the old, yet still pretty reliable, machinery—a job he thrives on!

Cider has its beginnings in the harvest of handpicked New York State Apple Country apples. Once picked and delivered to the Mill, the apples are stored at 38°F until pressing. As cider pressing begins, they are sent through the apple washer located

The original turbine still in use at the Fly Creek Cider Mill is located 12 feet underneath the Mill to take advantage of water flowing by gravity from the pond in the back into Fly Creek at the front of the Mill. A millrace is a channel by which water travels to and from the turbine.

1: Hand-picked, New York State-grown apples are dumped to be washed before pressing. **2:** Apples traveling into the apple washer. **3:** Ground apples being leveled in a frame containing nylon cloth. This process is called laying up a cheese. **4:** 32 bushels of ground apples are sandwiched in the cheese between plastic racks. **5:** Turning the pressing tray to place the cheese under the 1889 Boomer & Boschert press. **6:** The press's water-powered, water-hydraulic pump creates 2,000 pounds of pressure per square inch. **7:** Pressing takes about 30 minutes, creating almost 100 gallons of cider. **8:** Cider is bottled for visitors. **9:** Remaining apple pulp called pomace is spread on a local field as fertilizer and offered to local farmers as feed.

in the Mill's old icehouse where they are scrubbed with nine rows of brushes and heavy jets of fresh, clean water. The washing is immediately followed by grinding, which is done through the power of the Mill's 1924 Waterloo Boy two-cylinder engine (which was purchased in 1924 directly from the factory that later became the John Deere Company). The Waterloo Boy runs a flat belt that turns a line shaft delivering power to the grinder. Once ground, the apple mash, called pomace, is transferred to the 1889 Boomer & Boschert water-hydraulic press. Layers of pomace are placed in nylon cloths between plastic racks in a formation called a "cheese." After the cheese is complete, the entire pressing tray is rotated under the press. Pressure is applied by a two-cylinder water pump that is powered by the Lesner Water Turbine located deep in the basement of the Mill. The spinning turbine runs another flat belt to transfer power to the press's water-hydraulic pump creating pressure on the cheese. The resulting sweet cider is pressed out of the pomace and held in a storage tank for the next step: assuring cider safety.

The newest piece of technology at the Mill is an ultraviolet light–processing machine called Cidersure that ensures the best cider possible. The Cidersure process guarantees cider safety by shining high-intensity ultraviolet light through a very thin stream of cider. The light eliminates the possibility of any harmful contaminates in the fresh juice. This sweet cider is then pumped into two storage tanks and is ready to be tasted and purchased by Mill visitors.

The 1889 Boomer & Boschert press still makes all the Mill's cider. Considered state-of-the-art technology at the time, the water-hydraulic press was faster and more powerful than traditional screw-type presses.

Here's the difference between apple cider and apple juice: Apple cider is picked, washed, ground, and pressed fresh juice. Apple juice starts out as cider and is then concentrated into a syrup or a powder, which is reconstituted with water and hermetically bottled to be shelf stable.

From cider making, it is not a far reach to create highly alcoholic spirits from apple juice. If stored at low temperature, the sweet cider will begin to ferment and hard, alcoholic cider will result. This can be done either naturally, using the wild yeasts that it contains, or through the addition of other yeasts. Early on, Americans developed a taste for the hard stuff. In the 1700s, a firm started in New Jersey by a Scotsman, Alexander Laird, was making distilled spirits from apple juice. It is said that these "cyder spirits," or applejack, warmed the troops fighting the British under George Washington's command. Although we don't make spirits at the Mill, we have developed apple wines and hard ciders that are made for us by licensed distilleries and are sold in our Mill store.

Apples for Cider

Cider making requires a mix of apples of differing tannin content and acidity to create the balance of flavor the cider maker desires. Sweet ciders are generally pressed from apples low in tannins and acidity, such as Golden Delicious, and hard ciders from those high in tannins and acidity, such as heirlooms like Kingston Black.

At the Mill, we use a blend of those apples available to us—a mix of those from our own tiny orchard with those from neighboring orchards—so each week's cider has a slightly different flavor. We start pressing with at least four different varieties and then blend in up to eight or nine, making a darker, richer cider as the process goes on. To us, it resembles wine making in that the cider maker has the same control of flavor as does the winemaker in their decisions about the variety and amount of fruit to use. Although each year brings new varieties to our attention, we have had the most success using McIntoshes, Paula Reds, Jonagolds, Empires, Macouns, Golden Supremes, Northern Spies, Galas, Crispins, and Fujis.

Apples are fat, sodium, and cholesterol free, and most have no more than 80 calories each. Plus, eating a raw apple after a meal removes almost 95 percent of the bacteria that causes tooth decay.

Basic Recipes

Fly Creek Cider Mill 1856 Barbecue Sauce

MAKES ABOUT 6 CUPS

2 tablespoons corn oil

1 cup finely minced onion

3 cups ketchup

¾ cup light brown sugar

¾ cup apple cider vinegar

½ cup beer

½ cup hard cider

3 tablespoons
Worcestershire sauce

1½ tablespoons chili powder

1 tablespoon pure maple
syrup

2 teaspoons mustard
powder

Salt and pepper, to taste

Tabasco sauce, to taste

1. Heat the oil in a large, heavy-bottomed saucepan over medium heat. Add the onion and cook, stirring frequently, for 5 minutes, or until soft.

2. Add the ketchup, brown sugar, vinegar, beer, cider, Worcestershire sauce, chili powder, maple syrup, and mustard powder, stirring to blend well. Season with the salt, pepper, and Tabasco sauce, and bring to a simmer. Cook at a bare simmer for 40 minutes, or until the flavors have blended. Taste and, if necessary, adjust the seasoning.

3. Remove from the heat and set aside to cool. When cool, store tightly covered, in a refrigerator for up to 1 month.

Spice Rub for Meats and Poultry

MAKES ABOUT ¾ CUP

¼ cup light brown sugar

¼ cup paprika

1 tablespoon onion powder

2 teaspoons freshly ground
black pepper

1 teaspoon garlic powder

1 teaspoon mustard powder

1 teaspoon ground cumin

1 teaspoon pure chile
powder

1 teaspoon celery salt

1 teaspoon cayenne pepper
or to taste

1. Combine the brown sugar and paprika in a small mixing bowl or glass container with a lid. Add the onion powder, pepper, garlic powder, mustard powder, cumin, chile powder, celery salt, and cayenne. Whisk together to combine in a bowl, or shake in a jar, to blend completely.

2. Store, covered, in a cool, dark spot for up to 6 months. Use as a dry rub on beef, pork, or any type of poultry that is to be grilled or roasted.

Apple Cider Vinaigrette

MAKES ABOUT 1½ CUPS

¾ cup apple cider

3 tablespoons apple cider vinegar

1 teaspoon Dijon mustard

1 teaspoon minced flat-leaf parsley

1 cup olive oil

Salt and pepper, to taste

1. Place the apple cider in a small saucepan over high heat and bring to a boil. Boil for 8 minutes, or until reduced to 3 tablespoons. Remove from the heat and set aside to cool.

2. When the cider is cool, transfer it to a glass jar with a lid. Add the vinegar, mustard, and parsley. Cover and shake to blend. Uncover and add the oil, salt, and pepper. Cover again and shake well to emulsify.

3. Serve immediately or refrigerate for up to 1 week. Bring to room temperature and shake before using.

NOTE: *This is an excellent vinaigrette for any tossed green, vegetable, or fruit salad. It's also a terrific seasoning or sauce poured over warm sautéed bitter greens, such as kale, chard, mustard greens, or chicory, or over grilled pork chops or chicken.*

Spicy Apple Vinaigrette

MAKES ABOUT 1½ CUPS

½ cup olive oil

½ cup walnut oil (see note)

¼ cup chopped fresh ginger

1 small hot chile, stemmed, seeded, and cut into small pieces

1 large tart apple, peeled, cored, and cut into small pieces

¼ cup apple cider vinegar

2 tablespoons white miso paste

Freshly grated zest of 1 lemon

Cayenne pepper, to taste

Salt, to taste

1. Heat the oils in a small frying pan over low heat. Add the ginger and chile and cook, stirring frequently, for 10 minutes, or until the oil is nicely flavored. Remove from the heat and strain through a fine mesh sieve, discarding the ginger and chile. Set aside.

2. Combine the apple with the vinegar, miso paste, lemon zest, and cayenne in a blender and process until smooth.

3. With the motor running, add the oil mixture and salt. Process until just emulsified.

4. Serve or cover and refrigerate for up to 3 days. Bring to room temperature before serving.

NOTE: *If you don't have walnut oil on hand, you can use only olive oil or any other vegetable oil. This is an excellent vinaigrette for slaws or fruit salads, or as a sauce for grilled chicken, pork, or fish.*

31

Mulling Spice Mix

MAKES ABOUT 1¼ CUPS

6 cinnamon sticks

2 whole nutmeg

3 tablespoons cardamom pods

4 whole star anise

¼ cup whole allspice berries

¼ cup whole cloves

¼ cup dried orange *or* lemon peel

3 tablespoons black peppercorns

1. Combine the cinnamon sticks, nutmeg, and cardamom pods in the bowl of a food processor fitted with the metal blade attachment. Process, using quick on-and-off turns, just until the spices are broken into pieces.

2. Combine the broken spices with the star anise, allspice, cloves, citrus peel, and peppercorns in a glass jar with a lid. Cover and shake to blend.

3. When ready to serve, place ¼ cup of the spice mix in a small cotton drawstring bag or a double piece of cheesecloth. If using the cheesecloth, form it into a bag and tie it firmly closed with kitchen twine. You should have enough mix to make 4 to 5 bags.

4. Place the bags in an airtight container and store in a cool, dark spot for up to 6 months.

It is a good idea to make tags for the mulling spice bags that list the ingredients as well as the directions for making mulled cider. These little bags make great last-minute house gifts.

MULLED CIDER

Combine 1 bag of spice mix with 1 quart apple cider in a nonreactive saucepan over medium heat. Bring to a simmer and simmer for 5 minutes. Remove from the heat, remove and discard the spice mix bag, and pour the hot cider into mugs. Garnish with a long cinnamon stick and a slice of crisp apple, or sprinkle the top with ground cinnamon or nutmeg.

32

Apple Butter

8 pounds apples, both tart and sweet kinds, washed, stemmed, and quartered

1 quart apple cider

⅓ cup light brown sugar for each cup cooked fruit

Juice and freshly grated zest of 1 lemon

1 tablespoon ground cinnamon *or* to taste

2 teaspoons ground allspice

1 teaspoon ground cloves

1. Combine the apples with the cider in a large, heavy-bottomed saucepan over medium–high heat. Cover and bring to a simmer. Lower the heat and cook at a bare simmer, stirring occasionally to keep the fruit from sticking, for 15 minutes, or until very soft. Remove from the heat.

2. Either press the hot fruit through a fine mesh strainer or through a food mill into a clean mixing bowl, discarding the skins and seeds.

3. When all of the fruit has been puréed, measure and transfer to a clean, heavy-bottomed saucepan. For each cup of fruit, add ⅓ cup brown sugar. Stir in the lemon juice and zest along with the cinnamon, allspice, and cloves.

4. Place over low heat and cook, stirring constantly, until the sugar has dissolved completely. Continue to cook, stirring frequently, for 30 minutes, or until the apple butter is very thick and spreadable.

5. While the butter is cooking, place a rack on the bottom of a pot made specifically for canning or a cooking pot large enough to hold the number of jars you are going to process completely submerged in water. Add water and bring to boil over high heat.

6. Remove the butter from the heat and immediately ladle into clean sterilized canning jars leaving ½-inch headspace in each filled jar. Remove air bubbles from jars by pushing around edge of jar with a rubber spatula. Wipe sealing edges clean with a dry cloth. Place lid and cap on each jar and twist closed. Do not seal tightly.

33

If canning is too much trouble, you can place the Apple Butter in clean, sterilized containers, preferably jars, with tight-fitting lids and refrigerate for up to 2 weeks or freeze for up to 3 months.

NOTE: *Apple Butter is a delicious spread for toast, cheese sandwiches, pancakes, or waffles, or as a glaze for grilled or roasted pork or poultry.*

APPLE BUTTER (CONTINUED)

7. Place the filled jars on the rack at the bottom of the pot, allowing free circulation of the boiling water around and under each jar. The water must be at least three inches above tops of jars (add water if necessary). Bring to a boil as quickly as possible. When water is at a vigorous boil, begin counting off 10 minutes of processing time.

8. When processing time is reached, using tongs, remove jars from boiling water bath. Complete the seal by holding each jar with a kitchen towel and tightening the screw cap. Turn the jars upside down for 10 minutes. Then, set the jars upright and place about 2 inches apart on wire racks or newspaper, away from drafts, to cool.

9. When cool, label with name and date and place in a cool dark spot for up to 1 year.

34

Cider Syrup

MAKES ABOUT 2 CUPS

4 cups apple cider

1¼ cups packed light brown sugar

5 tablespoons plus 1 teaspoon unsalted butter

1 tablespoon apple cider vinegar

1 teaspoon fresh lemon juice

1. Combine the cider, brown sugar, butter, vinegar, and lemon juice in a medium nonreactive saucepan over medium heat. Cook at a low simmer for 30 minutes, or until syrupy and reduced by half.

2. Remove from the heat and cool slightly before using. Store, covered, in a refrigerator for up to 2 weeks.

NOTE: *This syrup is great on pancakes, waffles, ice cream, or as a sweetener for teas.*

35

Hard-Cider Sauce

MAKES ABOUT 2 CUPS

3 cups hard cider

1 cup Apple Butter
(see page 33) *or* other fine
quality apple butter

½ cup light brown sugar

¼ cup honey

1 teaspoon fresh
lemon juice

¼ teaspoon salt

6 tablespoons unsalted
butter

2 tablespoons applejack
brandy (optional)

1. Combine the cider, apple butter, brown sugar, honey, lemon juice, and salt in a medium, heavy-bottomed saucepan over medium heat. Bring to a simmer, stirring frequently. Raise the heat and bring to a boil. Boil, stirring constantly, for 10 minutes, or until the mixture has reduced by half and has thickened just a bit.

2. Stir in the butter and return to a boil. Immediately remove from the heat and stir in the brandy, if using.

3. Remove from the heat and serve. Or, scrape into a nonreactive container, set aside to cool, and serve at room temperature. Sauce can be covered and refrigerated. Reheat before using.

NOTE: *This can be used as a sauce for cakes, ice cream, or for pork roast or chicken.*

Mill-Aged Cheddar Pie Pastry

MAKES ENOUGH FOR 2 BOTTOM-CRUST PIES
OR 1 DOUBLE CRUST PIE

1¼ cups all-purpose flour, sifted

1 teaspoon salt

1⅓ cups grated New York State Fly Creek Cider Mill Mill-aged Cheddar cheese *or* other fine quality Cheddar cheese

1½ sticks unsalted butter, chilled and cut into small pieces

1. Place the flour and salt in the bowl of a food processor fitted with the metal blade attachment. Process to blend. Add the cheese and butter and process, using quick on-and-off turns, to a coarse meal. Then, process for just a few seconds more, or until the dough comes together.

2. Remove the dough from the bowl and, using your hands, form it into 2 disks of equal size. Wrap each one in plastic film and refrigerate for an hour to firm.

3. When ready to use, unwrap and lightly flour each disk. Roll each disk out between 2 pieces of wax or parchment paper to 10-inch rounds. The dough will be sticky, so handle carefully.

NOTE: *Use as you would other pie pastry, but it is particularly delicious when combined with apple, pear, or mincemeat pie fillings or for savory pies, such as our Apple–Cheddar Quiche (see page 129), Fly Creek Apple–Cheddar Pie (see page 158), or chicken or pork pot pies.*

37

Breakfast

Fly Creek Cider Mill Apple Cider Doughnuts

MAKES 18 DOUGHNUTS

1 cup apple cider

2 cups granulated sugar (divided)

2 teaspoons apple *or* pumpkin pie spice mix (divided)

3½ cups all-purpose flour, sifted

1 tablespoon baking powder

1¼ teaspoons baking soda

½ teaspoon salt

2 large eggs, room temperature

½ cup buttermilk

6 tablespoons unsalted butter, melted

Approximately 2½ quarts vegetable oil, for frying

1. Place the cider in a small nonreactive saucepan over medium heat. Bring to a boil; then, lower the heat and simmer until reduced to ⅓ cup. Remove from the heat and set aside to cool.

2. Combine 1 cup of the sugar with 1 teaspoon of the spice mix in a shallow bowl. Set aside.

3. Combine the remaining 1 cup of sugar with the flour, baking powder, baking soda, remaining spice mix, and salt in a large mixing bowl.

4. Combine the cooled cider with the eggs, buttermilk, and melted butter in a small mixing bowl. When fully blended, stir the liquid into the dry ingredients, mixing until combined. The dough will be sticky.

5. Generously flour a clean, flat work surface.

6. Scrape the dough onto the floured surface. Lightly flour your hands and pat the dough out into a circle that is 13 inches around and ⅓-inch thick.

7. Using a doughnut cutter (a round cutter with a hole in the center), cut out as many doughnuts as possible. Repeat the process with any remaining scraps once; after one repeat, discard remaining scraps since the dough will become tough if worked too much.

8. Place the oil in a deep fat fryer over medium heat, and bring to 370°F on a candy thermometer.

FLY CREEK CIDER MILL APPLE CIDER DOUGHNUTS (CONTINUED)

9. Using a spatula, carefully transfer a few doughnuts to the hot oil. Do not crowd the pan. The doughnuts should rise to the surface as they begin to cook. Fry, turning once, for 3 minutes, or until light and golden brown. Using a slotted spatula, transfer the doughnuts to a double layer of paper towel to drain.

10. Continue frying until a few doughnuts at a time until all of the dough has been used.

11. Let the doughnuts cool for a couple of minutes. Then, transfer one at a time to the dish of the spiced sugar mixture and turn to coat lightly. Serve warm or at room temperature.

We sell thousands upon thousands of our cider doughnuts each season, and at the opening of every one, we are astonished at the continuing demand for them. We do ship them all across the country, but it seems that the combination of place and dough-nut is the most appealing.

Apple Pie Spice Pancakes
with Cider Syrup and Spiced Apples

1 cup whole-wheat flour

½ cup all-purpose flour

2 teaspoons baking powder

1 teaspoon apple pie spice mix

¼ teaspoon baking soda

Pinch salt

1½ cups buttermilk

1 large egg

2 tablespoons unsalted butter, melted

1 cup grated apples

Cider Syrup (see page 35)

Spiced Apples (recipe follows)

1. Combine the flours with the baking powder, spice mix, baking soda, and salt in a medium mixing bowl. Set aside.

2. Combine the buttermilk with the egg and melted butter in a small mixing bowl, whisking to blend well.

3. Using a wooden spoon, stir the liquid into the dry ingredients, mixing until just combined. Stir in the apples until just blended. Do not overmix, as this will cause the cooked pancakes to be tough. Set aside to rest for 10 minutes.

4. Place a nonstick skillet over medium heat. (A fine quality nonstick skillet will not require any greasing; however, if needed, lightly coat with melted butter, nonstick vegetable spray, or whatever fat you prefer.) Working with one at a time, ladle enough batter into the skillet to form cakes 3½ inches in diameter, leaving 2 inches between each cake.

5. Cook for 4 minutes, or until bubbles begin to form all over the top of the cakes. Turn and cook for another 3 minutes, or until cooked through and golden on both sides.

6. Remove from the heat. Serve hot with Cider Syrup and Spiced Apples, or with any syrup you like.

SPICED APPLES

1 cup apple cider

¼ cup dark brown sugar

1 tablespoon finely minced fresh ginger

1 teaspoon apple pie spice mix

4 cups peeled, thinly sliced tart apples

2 teaspoons cornstarch

2 teaspoons cold water

1 teaspoon fresh lemon juice

1. Combine the cider with the brown sugar, ginger, and spice mix in a medium saucepan over high heat, and bring to a boil. Stir in the apples and return to a simmer. Lower the heat and cook for 8 minutes, or until the apples are just barely tender.

2. Combine the cornstarch with the water in a small mixing bowl and then stir it into the apples. Add the lemon juice and cook for another 2 minutes, or until the sauce has thickened.

3. Remove from the heat and serve hot or at room temperature.

This might be called apple-overkill, but delicious flavors come together to make this spectacular breakfast or brunch treat. The syrup and the apples can also be used with cake or ice cream.

Puffy Apple Pancakes

MAKES 6 SERVINGS

2½ tablespoons unsalted butter, melted (divided), plus more for greasing

6 tablespoons light brown sugar (divided)

3 cups peeled, sliced tart-sweet apples (such as Honeycrisp)

2 large eggs, separated

¾ cup nonfat milk

1 teaspoon pure vanilla extract

½ cup all-purpose flour

Pinch salt

Confectioners' sugar, for dusting (optional)

1. Preheat the oven to 350°F.

2. Lightly butter the interior of 6 small soufflé dishes or custard cups. Set aside.

3. Combine 1 tablespoon of the melted butter with 2 tablespoons of the brown sugar in an 8-inch ovenproof nonstick skillet. Add the apples, tossing to coat, and place over medium heat. Cook, stirring frequently, for 10 minutes, or until the apples are nicely caramelized and golden brown. Remove from the heat and spoon an equal portion of the apples into each of the buttered dishes. Set aside.

4. Place the egg whites in a medium mixing bowl and, using a handheld electric mixer, beat on low to lighten. Raise the speed and beat for 2 minutes, or just until soft peaks form. Set aside.

5. Combine the remaining 1½ tablespoons of melted butter with the egg yolks, milk, and vanilla in a blender jar. Cover and process until just combined. Add the remaining 4 tablespoons of brown sugar along with the flour and salt and process until smooth. Pour the batter into the beaten egg whites, lifting and turning with a rubber spatula until the batter is almost completely blended into the whites. You should still see some small lumps of egg white.

6. Pour an equal portion of the batter over the apples in each dish. Place in the oven and bake for 15 minutes, or until the pancakes have risen and a cake tester inserted into the center comes out clean.

7. Remove from the oven and dust lightly with confectioners' sugar, if using. Serve immediately.

Sour Cream–Apple Coffee Cake

MAKES 1 13-INCH CAKE

2½ cups all-purpose flour

1 teaspoon baking powder

1 teaspoon baking soda

1 stick unsalted butter, room temperature

½ cup light brown sugar

½ cup granulated sugar

1 teaspoon pure vanilla extract

½ teaspoon salt

2 large eggs, room temperature

1 cup sour cream

2 cups peeled, finely diced tart apples

Optional Topping

½ cup chopped walnuts, peanuts, or pecans

½ cup firmly packed light brown sugar

1 teaspoon ground cinnamon

1. Preheat the oven to 375°F.

2. Coat the interior of a 13 × 9 × 2–inch baking pan or other 2-quart baking or cake pan with nonstick baking spray. Set aside.

3. Sift the flour, baking powder, and baking soda together. Set aside.

4. Place the butter in the bowl of a standing electric mixer fitted with the paddle attachment. Beat on low to soften. Add the brown and granulated sugars, vanilla, and salt and beat on medium until light and fluffy. Add the eggs, one at a time, occasionally scraping down the edge of the bowl with a rubber spatula.

5. With the motor running, alternately add the reserved dry ingredients and the sour cream to the creamed mixture, occasionally scraping down the edge of the bowl with a rubber spatula. When completely blended, remove the bowl from the mixer and, using the rubber spatula, fold the apples into the batter.

6. Scrape the batter into the prepared pan.

7. If using, prepare the topping. Combine the nuts with the brown sugar and cinnamon in a small mixing bowl, stirring with a fork to blend well. Sprinkle the topping evenly over the top of the batter.

8. Place the cake in the oven and bake for 30 minutes, or until a cake tester inserted into the center comes out clean.

9. Remove from the oven and transfer to a wire rack to cool for 10 minutes before serving. Serve warm or at room temperature.

10. Store, covered, at room temperature for up to 2 days.

NOTE: *Although the topping adds a nice crunch, it is not necessary. Plain or with a dusting of confectioners' sugar is absolutely delicious also.*

The Official New York State Apple Muffin

MAKES 24 MUFFINS

2 cups all-purpose flour

¾ cup light brown sugar

½ cup granulated sugar

2 teaspoons baking soda

1½ teaspoons ground cinnamon

½ teaspoon ground cloves

½ teaspoon salt

⅛ teaspoon ground nutmeg

2 cups coarsely chopped apples

½ cup golden raisins

½ cup chopped walnuts

3 large eggs, room temperature, lightly beaten

4 ounces cream cheese, cut into small pieces

1 stick unsalted butter, melted

1 teaspoon pure vanilla extract

Topping

½ cup light brown sugar

¼ cup all-purpose flour

1 teaspoon ground cinnamon

½ cup chopped walnuts

1 teaspoon freshly grated orange zest

2 tablespoons unsalted butter, melted

1. Preheat the oven to 375°F.

2. Line 2 12-cup, large muffin tins with paper liners. Set aside.

3. Combine the flour with the brown and granulated sugars, baking soda, cinnamon, cloves, salt, and nutmeg in a medium mixing bowl. Stir to blend completely. Set aside.

4. Combine the apples with the raisins and walnuts in another medium mixing bowl. Stir in the eggs, cream cheese, melted butter, and vanilla. When blended, begin adding the dry ingredients, a little at a time, stirring until just combined. Do not overmix.

5. Prepare the topping. Combine the brown sugar with the flour and cinnamon in a small mixing bowl, stirring to blend. Stir in the walnuts and orange zest and, when blended, stir in the melted butter.

6. Spoon an equal portion of the batter into the prepared muffin cups. Sprinkle an equal portion of the topping over each filled cup. Place in the oven and bake for 25 minutes, or until a cake tester inserted into the center of a couple of the muffins comes out clean.

This muffin, proudly honoring the state's apple crop, was created by elementary school children in North Syracuse, New York, and was officially adopted as the state muffin in 1987 through lobbying efforts of New York State school children. And, by the way, the apple is also the official New York State fruit.

7. Remove from the oven and transfer to a wire rack to cool.

8. When cool, store, tightly covered, at room temperature for up to 2 days.

49

Apple Breakfast Bars

MAKES ABOUT 12 BARS

1 stick unsalted butter, room temperature, plus more for greasing

½ cup light brown sugar

¼ cup honey

1½ cups rolled oats

½ cup ground almonds

¼ cup protein powder

1 teaspoon ground cinnamon

1 teaspoon freshly grated lemon zest

½ teaspoon baking powder

1 cup unsweetened applesauce

1. Preheat the oven to 350°F.

2. Generously coat the interior of an 8-inch square baking pan with butter. Set aside.

3. Combine the stick of butter with the brown sugar and honey in a medium saucepan over low heat. Cook, stirring constantly with a wooden spoon, for 4 minutes, or until the butter has melted and the mixture is blended completely. Remove from the heat.

4. While the mixture is hot, add the oats, almonds, protein powder, cinnamon, lemon zest, and baking powder, stirring constantly. When blended, add the applesauce and beat until completely incorporated.

5. Spoon the batter into the prepared pan, smoothing the top with a spatula. Place in the oven and bake for 15 minutes, or until golden brown and the edges begin to pull away from the pan.

6. Remove from the oven and transfer to a wire rack to cool. When cool, transfer to the refrigerator for 1 hour, or until chilled. This is important as it keeps the bars from crumbling when being cut.

7. Remove from the refrigerator and carefully invert the pan onto a clean cutting board. Using a serrated knife, cut into rectangles 1 inch wide and however long you desire.

You can cut these into small squares and use them for an afternoon candy-like treat.

Apple–Pecan Muffins

MAKES 12 MUFFINS

2 cups all-purpose flour

2 teaspoons baking soda

1 teaspoon ground cinnamon

½ teaspoon ground ginger

½ teaspoon salt

2 large eggs, room temperature

1 cup granulated sugar

½ cup canola oil

2 teaspoons pure vanilla extract

4 cups peeled, diced tart apples (see note)

1 cup pecan pieces

1. Preheat the oven to 350°F.

2. Line a 12-cup, large muffin tin with paper liners. Set aside.

3. Sift the flour, baking soda, cinnamon, ginger, and salt together.

4. Place the eggs, sugar, oil, and vanilla in a medium mixing bowl, whisking vigorously to combine. Stir in the apples. Stir the sifted flour mixture into the apple mixture. When blended, stir in the pecans. The batter will be quite stiff.

5. Spoon an equal portion of the batter into each of the lined muffin cups.

6. Place in the oven and bake for 35 minutes, or until lightly browned around the edges and a cake tester inserted in the center comes out clean.

7. Remove from the oven and transfer to wire racks to cool slightly. Don't serve while still hot or the muffins will fall apart.

NOTE: *The apples should be cut into a ¾-inch dice.*

52

Starters
and Snacks

Apple Cider Jigglers

MAKES 1 9-INCH PAN, WHICH MAY BE CUT INTO AS
MANY PIECES OR SHAPES AS DESIRED

1 quart apple cider (divided)

4 envelopes unflavored gelatin

1. Place 3 cups of the cider into a medium saucepan over medium heat. Cook for 4 minutes, or just until it comes to a boil. Remove from the heat.

2. Meanwhile, place the remaining 1 cup of cider in a large mixing bowl. Sprinkle all of the gelatin into the cider and allow it to stand for 4 minutes. Pour the hot cider over the gelatin mixture, stirring with a wooden spoon until all of the gelatin has dissolved.

3. Pour the hot mixture into a 9-inch square pan. Place in the refrigerator and allow the mixture to chill for 8 hours, or until very firm.

4. When firm, remove from the refrigerator. Dip the pan into very hot water to loosen the gelatin. Using a sharp knife or small cookie cutters, cut the gelatin into shapes. Serve chilled. If you have any leftovers, be sure to return them to the refrigerator.

These are low-calorie, good-for-you treats that are even more special when you allow children to cut them into favorite shapes using small cookie cutters. Decorate the top with candies, flavored cream cheese, or anything appropriate for a birthday party or celebratory theme.

54

Hot Cheddar Cheese Dip

MAKES ABOUT 4 CUPS

2 cups fine quality
mayonnaise

1 cup grated fine quality
sharp Cheddar cheese

1 cup grated Gruyère *or*
fontina cheese

2 medium onions, peeled,
finely chopped

1 teaspoon hot paprika

1. Preheat the oven to 350°F.

2. Combine the mayonnaise with the Cheddar and Gruyère cheeses in a medium mixing bowl, stirring to blend. Add the onions and paprika and stir vigorously until the mixture is completely blended.

3. Scrape the mixture into a quart baking dish or casserole. Place in the oven and bake for 50 minutes, or until bubbling and golden on the top and around the edges.

4. Remove from the oven and serve hot with crackers, toasts, or sliced baguette.

Zesty Cheese Pot

MAKES ABOUT 3 CUPS

1 pound fine quality
Cheddar cheese, chopped
into small pieces

1 tablespoon Dijon mustard

1 tablespoon dried onion
flakes

1 teaspoon curry powder

1 teaspoon chopped fresh
chives

½–⅔ cup hard cider

Cayenne pepper, to taste

1. Place the cheese in the bowl of a standing electric mixer fitted with the paddle attachment. Add the mustard, onion flakes, curry powder, and chives. Turn the mixer to medium–low speed and beat to just blend. Add ⅓ cup of the cider and beat until well incorporated. If the mixture seems too thick, add additional cider as needed. It should be thick enough to coat a cracker or pita crisp without being runny. Add cayenne pepper.

2. Place the cheese mixture in a decorative crock and refrigerate until ready to serve.

3. Serve in the crock along with New York State apples, crackers, pita, toasts, or raisin–walnut bread.

Sweet Corn Salsa–Black Bean Dip

MAKES ABOUT 2 CUPS

1 (15½-ounce) can black beans, rinsed and drained

1 cup Fly Creek Cider Mill Sweet Corn Salsa *or* other high quality corn salsa

2 tablespoons minced fresh cilantro

1 teaspoon minced garlic

Juice of 1 lime

Hot sauce, to taste

1. Combine the beans with the salsa, cilantro, and garlic in a medium mixing bowl. Add the lime juice and hot sauce and stir to blend.

2. Cover and refrigerate for 30 minutes to allow flavors to blend.

3. Serve chilled with tortilla chips, pita bread, or crackers.

NOTE: *This mix also makes a very tasty side salad.*

57

Nutty Apple Slices

MAKES ABOUT 40 APPLE SLICES

1 (8-ounce) package cream cheese, room temperature

½ cup packed light brown sugar

1 teaspoon pure vanilla extract

2¼ cups chopped dry-roasted peanuts

4 large tart apples, washed, cored, and cut into medium slices (see note)

1. Place the cream cheese in a small mixing bowl. Using a handheld electric mixer, beat until very soft. Add the brown sugar and vanilla and beat until light and fluffy. Scrape the beaters clean with a rubber spatula.

2. Using the spatula, fold the peanuts into the cream cheese mixture until thoroughly blended.

3. Spoon a heaping teaspoon of the cream cheese mixture onto each apple slice. Arrange the slices on a decorative platter and serve.

NOTE: *When peeling or cutting apples in advance of use, always place the peeled or cut pieces in cold water with the juice of 1 lemon. The acid in the lemon keeps the peeled or cut area from discoloring. Always drain and pat the pieces dry before using.*

You can make the cream cheese mixture and store it, covered and refrigerated, for up to 1 week. You can keep it on hand for apple, pear, or celery snacks throughout the week.

Barbecued Chicken Wings

MAKES 1½ POUNDS

1½ pounds chicken wings, end tips removed and each wing cut into 2 pieces at the joint

1½ cups Fly Creek Cider Mill 1856 Barbecue Sauce (see page 28) *or* barbecue sauce of your choice

2 cups unflavored breadcrumbs

½ teaspoon cayenne pepper *or* to taste

Salt, to taste

1. Preheat the oven to 375°F.

2. Line 2 baking sheets with aluminum foil. Set aside.

3. Combine the chicken wings with the barbecue sauce in a large mixing bowl. Toss to coat each wing well. Set aside.

4. Combine the breadcrumbs with the cayenne pepper and salt in a resealable plastic bag.

5. Working with a few pieces at a time, place the barbecue-sauced wings in the breadcrumb mixture, tossing gently to coat; you don't want to lose any of the sauce off the wings.

6. After coating, lay the wings on the prepared baking sheets.

7. When all of the wings are coated, place in the oven and bake for 25 minutes, or until cooked through, golden brown, and crispy.

8. Serve hot or at room temperature with extra barbecue sauce for dipping, if desired.

59

Thai Chicken–Apple Skewers

MAKES 6 SERVINGS

1 cup unsweetened coconut milk

¼ cup fresh lime juice

3 tablespoons Thai red curry paste (see note)

3 tablespoons chopped cilantro

2 tablespoons peanut oil

1 teaspoon freshly grated ginger

1 teaspoon freshly grated lemon zest

1½ pounds boneless, skinless chicken breasts, cut into chunks

2 tart apples, peeled, cored, and cut into chunks

1 pint basket cherry tomatoes

Salt, to taste

1. Combine the coconut milk, lime juice, curry paste, cilantro, peanut oil, ginger, and lemon zest in a small mixing bowl, stirring to blend well. Set aside.

2. Place the chicken in a large resealable plastic bag. Add the liquid mixture, seal the bag, and gently toss to coat well. Refrigerate for 1 to 6 hours to allow flavors to penetrate the chicken.

3. If using bamboo skewers, place them in cold water to cover for at least 1 hour. This will keep them from burning once on the grill.

4. When ready to cook, preheat and oil the grill or preheat a stovetop grill pan. Or, if you have neither, heat a large nonstick frying pan.

5. Remove the marinated chicken from the refrigerator and carefully begin threading onto the wet skewers, alternating the chicken chunks, apple pieces, and tomatoes. Each skewer should have at least 2 pieces each of the apple and tomato and 3 pieces of chicken, beginning and ending with chicken. Season with salt. Do not discard the marinade.

6. Place the skewers on the hot grill and cook, turning frequently and basting with the marinade, for 7 minutes, or until the chicken is cooked through and the apple and tomato are beginning to color.

7. Remove from the heat and serve.

NOTE: *Thai curry paste is available at Asian and specialty food markets as well as at many supermarkets and online.*

60

Turkey and Apple Salsa Roll-up

MAKES 1 ROLL-UP

1 flatbread *or* flour tortilla

3 ounces sliced roast turkey

¼ cup Fly Creek Apple Salsa (recipe follows), plus more, if desired

¼ cup diced avocado

Shredded iceberg lettuce, for sprinkling

1. Lay the flatbread out on a clean work surface. Place the turkey slices on top, leaving an inch all around the edge uncovered. Spoon the salsa over the turkey, followed by the avocado and lettuce.

2. Fold 2 opposing sides of the bread over the filling and then roll the entire bread up and over the filling to completely enclose.

3. Serve immediately with additional Fly Creek Apple Salsa on the side, if desired.

FLY CREEK APPLE SALSA

MAKES ABOUT 5 CUPS

2 Crispin apples, peeled,
cored, and diced

2 cloves garlic, peeled
and minced

3 cups seeded and chopped
ripe tomatoes

1 cup finely chopped
red onion

1 jalapeño chile, trimmed,
seeded, and minced

½ cup canned chopped
green chilies, drained

¼ cup chopped fresh
cilantro

¼ cup red wine vinegar

2 tablespoons olive oil

TO SERVE RAW:

1. Combine the apples, garlic, tomatoes, and onion in a large mixing bowl, stirring to blend. When blended, stir in the jalapeño, chopped chilies, cilantro, vinegar, and olive oil. Let stand for at least 30 minutes to allow the flavors to meld and even out.

2. Serve at room temperature or cover and refrigerate for up to 2 weeks.

TO SERVE COOKED:

1. Place all of the ingredients in a heavy saucepan over medium heat. Cook, stirring frequently, for 12 minutes, or until just boiling.

2. Remove from the heat and set aside to cool. Serve as above.

NOTES: *If desired, this salsa may be processed for canning. Follow your usual canning process or see page 33.*

Serve as a condiment on sandwiches or with grilled meat or poultry or as a dip with chips.

63

Easy Bacon–Apple Pizza

MAKES 2 9-INCH PIZZAS

2 (9-inch) flatbread pizza crusts

3 tablespoons extra virgin olive oil

2 cups (about 8 ounces) shredded fine quality Cheddar cheese

2 tart apples, peeled, cored, and cut lengthwise into very thin slices

¾ pound smoky bacon, cooked, drained, and crumbled

½ cup grated Parmesan cheese

2 cups arugula, tough stems removed (optional)

1. Preheat the broiler.

2. Warm the pizza crusts according to the manufacturer's suggestion.

3. Place the warm pizza crusts on a baking sheet. Using a pastry brush, generously coat each warm pizza crust with olive oil. Evenly sprinkle an equal portion of the Cheddar cheese over the top of each crust followed by an equal portion of the apple slices arranged on top. Then, sprinkle an equal portion of the bacon over each one. Lightly sprinkle the Parmesan over each crust and place in the broiler.

4. Broil for 3 minutes, or until the cheese has melted and is bubbling. Remove from the broiler and, if using, sprinkle an equal portion of the arugula over the top of each hot pizza.

5. Serve immediately.

64

Apple Popovers

MAKES 12 POPOVERS

3 tart-sweet apples, peeled, cored, and cut lengthwise into 8 slices each

½ cup packed light brown sugar

½ teaspoon ground cinnamon

½ teaspoon ground cloves

4 tablespoons unsalted butter, melted (divided), plus more for greasing

2 large eggs, room temperature

1 cup nonfat milk

1 cup all-purpose flour, sifted

2 teaspoons granulated sugar

3 tablespoons cinnamon-sugar

1. Preheat the oven to 425°F.

2. Generously butter the interior of a 12-cup muffin tin. Set aside.

3. Combine the apples, brown sugar, cinnamon, and cloves with 2 tablespoons of the melted butter in a medium nonstick frying pan over medium heat. Cook, stirring frequently, for 15 minutes, or until the apples have softened slightly but still hold their shape. Remove from the heat and set aside to cool.

4. While the apples are cooling, make the batter. Combine the eggs and milk in a medium mixing bowl, whisking to blend completely. Whisk in the flour, the sugar, and remaining 2 tablespoons of the melted butter, whisking until very smooth.

5. Place 2 slices of cooked apple in the bottom of each greased muffin cup. Place in the oven for 2 minutes, or just until the pan is hot. Remove from the oven and ladle an equal portion of the batter into each cup, filling until ¾ full. Sprinkle an equal portion of the cinnamon-sugar over the top of each popover.

6. Place in the oven and bake for 10 minutes. Reduce the heat to 375°F and continue to bake for an additional 15 minutes, or until the popovers have risen and are light and golden brown.

7. Remove from the oven. You can either lift the popover out and serve it right-side up or invert so that the apple slices are on top. Either way, the popovers should be served hot.

66

Cinnamon–Cider Candy Apples

MAKES 8 CANDY APPLES

8 small crisp apples, washed and dried

1 cup granulated sugar

¼ cup white corn syrup

¼ cup cold water

¾ cup half-and-half, room temperature

¼ cup apple cider

1 teaspoon cinnamon extract

¾ cup chopped peanuts

¾ cup chopped lightly salted pretzels

1. Stick a wooden craft stick into the stem end of each of the apples. Set aside.

2. Line a baking sheet with parchment paper or aluminum foil. Set aside.

3. Combine the sugar and corn syrup with the water in a heavy-bottomed nonstick saucepan over high heat. Cook, stirring constantly, for 3 minutes, or until the sugar has dissolved completely. Bring to a boil, lower the heat to medium–high, and cook, without stirring, for 10 minutes, or until the caramel is golden brown and thick.

4. Add the half-and-half, cider, and cinnamon extract to the hot caramel. Bring to a simmer, lower the heat to a gentle simmer, and cook, stirring frequently, for 10 minutes, or until it registers 235°F on a candy thermometer.

5. While the caramel is cooking, combine the peanuts and pretzels in a bowl large enough to allow you to dip the apples into it. Set aside.

6. Place the pan holding the hot caramel into a larger pan filled with boiling water.

7. Working with 1 apple at a time and holding it by the craft stick, swirl the apple in the hot caramel. Then, immediately dip the caramel into the nut mixture to lightly coat. Once dipped and coated with the nut mixture, place the apple on the prepared baking sheet and let cool.

8. When all of the apples have been dipped and cooled, store in a single layer, at room temperature, for up to 3 days.

Soups and Salads

Baked Cider–Onion Soup

MAKES 8 SERVINGS

3 tablespoons unsalted butter

2 teaspoons light brown sugar

1 pound red onions, peeled and cut lengthwise into thin strips

1 pound sweet white onions, peeled and cut lengthwise into thin strips

Salt and pepper, to taste

1 tablespoon all-purpose flour

8 cups low-sodium, nonfat chicken broth

2 cups water

½ cup apple cider

8 thick slices white toast

8 thick slices Gruyère, Swiss, or fontina cheese

1. Heat the butter in a large soup pot over medium heat. Add the brown sugar, stirring to blend. Add the onions, salt, and pepper and cook, stirring frequently, for 15 minutes, or until the onions are nicely colored. Stir in the flour and cook for 1 minute, or until the flour has blended into the liquid.

2. Add the chicken broth, water, and cider, stirring to blend. Bring to a simmer, then lower the heat and cook at a gentle simmer for 90 minutes.

3. Preheat the broiler.

4. Place 8 ceramic soup bowls on a baking sheet with sides. Ladle an equal portion of the soup into each bowl. Lay a piece of the toast on top of each soup-filled bowl. Top with a slice of the cheese.

5. Place under the broiler for 3 minutes, or until the cheese has melted and is golden brown.

6. Remove from the broiler and serve immediately with extra toasts or sliced baguette for sopping up the broth.

69

Apple–Pumpkin Soup

MAKES ABOUT 3 QUARTS

2 tablespoons unsalted butter

1½ cups chopped onion

1 teaspoon minced garlic

3 (15-ounce) cans pumpkin purée

1 cup Apple Butter (see page 33) *or* other fine quality apple butter

4 cups low-sodium, nonfat chicken broth

1 cup apple cider

2 tablespoons curry powder

Salt and pepper, to taste

1 cup heavy cream

¼ cup sour cream (optional)

1. Melt the butter in a large soup pot over medium heat. Add the onion and garlic and cook, stirring frequently, for 4 minutes, or until softened.

2. Stir in the pumpkin and apple butter. Then, add the chicken broth and cider, stirring to blend well. Stir in the curry powder, salt, and pepper. Bring to a simmer.

3. Cook at a low simmer for 40 minutes, or until flavors have blended.

4. Remove from the heat and, working in batches, transfer to a blender and process to a smooth purée.

5. Place the purée in a clean saucepan. Add the cream and place over medium heat. Bring to just a simmer and immediately remove. Do not allow to boil.

6. Serve hot or cold with a dollop of sour cream on top, if using.

7. If serving cold, allow to cool and transfer to a covered container. Refrigerate until chilled or for up to 2 days.

This is a terrific holiday soup as it can be made ahead and it feeds a crowd. It is also deeply flavorful and full of zest—a great first course to get people talking about the meal.

Apple-Scented White Bean Soup

MAKES ABOUT 10 CUPS

2 (19-ounce) cans cannellini beans, drained and rinsed

1½ cups hard cider

3 carrots, peeled, trimmed, and finely diced

3 stalks celery, peeled, trimmed, and finely diced

3 cloves garlic, peeled and minced

1 medium red onion, peeled and finely diced

1 cup water

1 teaspoon dried thyme

Salt and pepper, to taste

1 tart apple, peeled, cored, and finely diced (optional)

1. Combine the beans and hard cider in a large soup pot. Stir in the carrots, celery, garlic, and onion along with the water. Season with the thyme, salt, and pepper.

2. Place pot over high heat. Bring mixture to a boil; then, lower the heat and simmer for 45 minutes, or until the beans are mushy and the vegetables very soft. If the soup gets too thick, you may need to add water or cider; the addition depends upon how deeply cider-flavored you want the finished soup to taste. Taste and, if necessary, add additional salt and pepper.

3. Remove soup from the heat and ladle into large, shallow bowls. Garnish the top with a sprinkle of apple dice, if using, and serve immediately.

Cheddar–Apple Soup

MAKES 4 BOWLS

2 tablespoons unsalted butter

2 tart apples, peeled, cored, and chopped

1 yellow onion, peeled and chopped

1 small russet potato, peeled and chopped

3 cups low-sodium, nonfat chicken broth

1½ cups apple cider *or* unsweetened apple juice

Salt and pepper, to taste

8 ounces fine quality Cheddar cheese (divided)

3 tablespoons (about 3 slices) crumbled cooked bacon

1 tablespoon minced fresh chives

1. Heat the butter in a soup pot over medium heat. Add the apples, onion, and potato and cook, stirring frequently, for 10 minutes, or until the apples and potato are softening.

2. Add the chicken broth and cider and season with the salt and pepper. Bring to a simmer and cook, stirring frequently, for 15 minutes, or until and apples and potato pieces are falling apart.

3. Add all but 2 tablespoons of the cheese, stirring until melted into the soup. Remove from the heat and, working in batches, purée the soup in a blender. Be sure to hold the lid down with a kitchen towel so that the hot liquid does not burst out of the blender jar.

4. Return the puréed soup to the pot, taste, and if necessary, season with additional salt and pepper. Bring to a simmer.

5. Remove the soup from the heat and ladle equal portions into 4 shallow bowls. Sprinkle with bacon, chives, and remaining cheese and serve immediately.

Cider Consommé

4 cups apple cider

Peels and cores from 3 apples

Skins from 2 red onions

2 cinnamon sticks

1 vanilla bean

1 (½-inch) piece ginger

1 teaspoon coriander seeds

3¾ cup water

½ apple, peeled and finely diced (optional)

Ground cinnamon, for garnish (optional)

1. Combine the cider with the apple peels and cores, onion skins, cinnamon sticks, vanilla bean, ginger, and coriander seeds in a large saucepan over medium heat. Add water and bring to a simmer. Lower the heat and cook at a bare simmer for 30 minutes or just until the liquid is infused with the spices.

2. Remove from the heat and let stand until cool.

3. Pour through a fine mesh sieve into a clean saucepan, discarding the solids. Return to medium heat and bring to simmer.

4. Remove from the heat and serve hot, garnished with apple dice and cinnamon, if using.

Cider Consommé is a great base for winter alcohol-based drinks, like toddies and mulled beverages. It can also be mixed with sparkling water or wine for a cocktail.

Winter Apple Salad

MAKES 6 TO 8 SERVINGS

1 (10-ounce) package baby spinach, washed, dried, and tough stems removed

2 tart apples, peeled, cored, and cut lengthwise into thin slices

1 medium red onion, peeled and cut lengthwise into thin slices

½ cup fresh orange juice

2 teaspoons fresh lemon juice

1 teaspoon honey

½ teaspoon chopped fresh thyme

1 cup olive oil

Salt and pepper, to taste

1. Combine the spinach, apple, and onion in a large salad bowl, tossing to blend. Set aside.

2. Combine the orange juice, lemon juice, honey, and thyme in a glass jar with a lid. Cover and shake well to blend. Uncover, add the olive oil, and season with the salt and pepper. Recover and shake very, very well to emulsify.

3. Pour just enough of the dressing over the salad to lightly coat, tossing to blend well.

4. Serve immediately with the extra dressing on the side.

Blue Cheese–Apple Slaw

MAKES 6 TO 8 SERVINGS

2 cups shredded green cabbage

2 cups shredded red cabbage

2 tart apples, peeled, cored, and cut lengthwise into thin slices

½ cup thinly sliced celery

¼ cup finely crumbled blue cheese (divided)

½ cup mayonnaise

2 tablespoons apple cider vinegar _or_ to taste

1 tablespoon granulated sugar _or_ to taste

Salt and pepper, to taste

1. Combine the cabbages with the apples and celery in a large mixing bowl, tossing to mix well. Sprinkle 1 tablespoon of the blue cheese over the top.

2. Combine the mayonnaise with the remaining 3 tablespoons of the blue cheese, the vinegar, and the sugar in a small mixing bowl. Using a kitchen fork, mash the cheese into the other ingredients. Season with the salt and pepper.

3. Pour the dressing over the cabbage mixture, tossing and turning to coat. Cover and refrigerate for 1 hour, or until chilled, tossing once or twice. Serve chilled with picnic fare or with roasted or grilled meats.

77

Molded Apple Cider Salad

MAKES 6 TO 8 SERVINGS

2 cups apple cider

½ cup cold water

2 envelopes unflavored gelatin

½ cup granulated sugar

⅓ cup fresh lemon juice

¼ teaspoon ground cloves

1 apple, peeled, cored, and diced

½ cup finely diced celery

½ cup chopped pecans

1. Place the cider in a small saucepan over medium heat and bring to a boil.

2. While the cider is coming to a boil, place the water in a small mixing bowl. Sprinkle the gelatin over the top and let stand for 1 minute.

3. Stir the softened gelatin into the boiling cider along with the sugar. Cook, stirring constantly, until the sugar has dissolved.

4. Remove from the heat and stir in the lemon juice and cloves. Pour the mixture into a large shallow container and transfer to the refrigerator. Chill for 1 hour.

5. Remove from the refrigerator and stir in the apples, celery, and pecans. Pour into a 1-quart serving bowl or decorative mold and return to the refrigerator.

6. Chill for at least 2 hours, or until very firm.

7. Serve chilled, as is or on a bed of lettuce or other salad greens.

If you chill this salad in a decorative mold, when ready to serve, dip the exterior into very hot water to loosen the gelatin. Unmold onto a serving platter or onto a bed of salad greens.

78

Chicken and Apple Salad

MAKES 6 SERVINGS

2 cups chopped cooked
chicken breast

¼ cup chopped scallions

¾ cup Fly Creek Apple Salsa
(see page 63)

¼ cup mayonnaise

¼ cup dried currants

2 tablespoons chopped
fresh parsley

6 cups chopped salad greens

2 tablespoons chopped
salted peanuts

1. Combine the chicken, scallions, salsa, and mayonnaise in the bowl of a food processor fitted with the metal blade attachment. Process, using quick on-and-off turns, until just combined. Do not overprocess or the mixture will be mushy.

2. Scrape the chicken mixture from the processor bowl into a medium mixing bowl. Add the currants and parsley and stir to mix.

3. Place a small mound of salad greens on each of 6 luncheon plates. Place a mound of the chicken mixture in the center of each salad. Sprinkle with peanuts and serve.

Brenda's Apple–Tuna Toss

MAKES 4 TO 6 BOWLS

4 cups shredded iceberg lettuce *or* 4 to 6 iceberg lettuce cups

1 (7-ounce) can tuna, packed in water

1 (11-ounce) can mandarin oranges, drained

2 cups peeled, diced apple

½ cup walnut pieces

2 teaspoons minced chives *or* scallion greens

½ cup mayonnaise

2 teaspoons soy sauce

1 teaspoon fresh lemon juice

1. Spread the lettuce evenly over a large platter. Alternately, place lettuce cups in the center of 4 to 6 small serving bowls. The latter works well for individual servings.

2. Combine the tuna with the oranges, apples, walnuts, and chives in a medium mixing bowl, tossing to blend evenly. Set aside.

3. Combine the mayonnaise, soy sauce, and lemon juice in a small mixing bowl, stirring to blend completely. Set aside.

4. If making 1 large salad, mound the tuna mixture in the center of the shredded lettuce, leaving a border of lettuce all around the edge. Drizzle the dressing over the top of the salad and serve immediately.

5. If making individual salads, pour the dressing over the tuna mixture, tossing to coat. Mound an equal portion of the tuna into the center of each lettuce cup and serve immediately.

Sides

Sautéed Brussels Sprouts with Apple and Pancetta

MAKES 6 SERVINGS

1 tablespoon olive oil

4 ounces diced pancetta (see note)

¼ cup minced shallots

1½ pounds brussels sprouts, trimmed and cut in half lengthwise

Salt and pepper, to taste

1 large tart apple, peeled, cored, and diced

1. Heat the olive oil in a large frying pan over medium heat. Add the pancetta and shallots and fry, stirring occasionally, for 10 minutes, or until the pancetta begins to crisp and the shallots take on some color.

2. Add the brussels sprouts to the pan, season with the salt and pepper, and cook, stirring occasionally, for 12 minutes, or until the sprouts are just about tender. Add the apple and continue to cook, stirring occasionally, for 5 additional minutes, or until the brussels sprouts are tender and the apple has some color.

3. Remove from the heat and serve.

NOTE: *Diced pancetta is available in the refrigerated section of many supermarkets and most specialty food stores. If unavailable, the pancetta may be replaced with 6 ounces (about 4 slices) of diced, smoked thick-sliced bacon.*

Apple Salsa–Baked Winter Squash

MAKES 6 SERVINGS

2 large butternut squash, peeled, seeded, and shredded

2 tart apples, peeled, cored, and shredded

1 medium onion, peeled and grated

1 teaspoon chopped fresh sage

1 cup Fly Creek Apple Salsa (see page 63)

Salt and pepper, to taste

4 tablespoons unsalted butter, melted, plus more for greasing

1. Preheat the oven to 350°F.

2. Lightly coat the interior of a 2-quart baking dish with butter.

3. Combine the squash, apples, onion, and sage in a large mixing bowl. When blended, add the salsa and stir to combine. Season with the salt and pepper.

4. Pour the mixture into the prepared baking dish. Pour the melted butter over the top and place in the oven.

5. Bake for 45 minutes, or until the squash is cooked through and golden brown and the sides are beginning to pull away from the pan.

6. Remove from the oven and serve hot.

Sweet and Sour Red Cabbage with Apples

MAKES 6 SERVINGS

4 tablespoons unsalted butter

½ cup diced red onion

1 (2-pound) red cabbage, trimmed, cored, and cut lengthwise into thick strips

2 Crispin *or* other tart apples, peeled, cored, and diced

Salt and pepper, to taste

¼ cup light brown sugar

⅔ cup balsamic vinegar

1. Heat the butter in a large, deep frying pan over medium heat. Add the onion and cook, stirring frequently, for 3 minutes, or until just softened. Add the cabbage and apple, season with the salt and pepper, and, using tongs, toss and turn to completely blend. Cook for 5 minutes, or until the cabbage has begun to wilt.

2. Lower the heat and sprinkle the top with the brown sugar followed by the vinegar. When the liquid begins to simmer, cover and cook, stirring from time to time, for 30 minutes, or until the cabbage is wilted completely and the flavors have blended.

3. Remove from the heat and serve.

Sautéed Spinach with Dried Apples and Pine Nuts

MAKES 6 SERVINGS

2 tablespoons olive oil

1 shallot, trimmed, peeled, and minced

1 clove garlic, peeled and minced

1 cup diced dried apple

½ cup pine nuts

3 tablespoons apple cider

1½ pounds baby spinach, tough stems removed

Salt and pepper, to taste

2 tablespoons grated Parmesan cheese

1. Heat the oil in a large frying pan over medium heat. Add the shallot and garlic and cook, stirring frequently, for 4 minutes, or just until softened. Add the apple, pine nuts, and cider and continue to cook, stirring frequently, for 5 minutes, or just until the apple has softened and the nuts have begun to color.

2. Add the spinach, salt, and pepper and cook, tossing and turning, for 3 minutes, or just until the spinach has wilted.

3. Transfer to a serving bowl, sprinkle with the cheese, and serve.

Cider Baked Beans

2 pounds dried Great Northern beans

1 cup diced onion

¼ pound salt pork, slab bacon, or smoked ham, diced

2 cups apple cider

1 cup dark brown sugar

½ cup ketchup

Salt and pepper, to taste

1. Place the beans in a large Dutch oven with cold water to cover by 2 inches. Set aside to soak for at least 8 hours or overnight. Drain well.

2. Return the soaked beans to the Dutch oven and again cover with cold water by 2 inches. Add the onion, place over high heat, and bring to a boil. Lower the heat and cook at a gentle simmer for 2 hours, or until the beans are tender. You may have to add water to keep the beans hydrated.

3. About 30 minutes before the beans are done, preheat the oven to 350°F.

4. Remove the pan from the heat and stir in the salt pork, cider, brown sugar, and ketchup. Cover and place in the oven.

5. Bake for 30 minutes. Uncover and taste. Add the salt and pepper, if necessary. Return the pan to the oven and cook, uncovered, for 1 hour, or until the beans are thick and the top is brown and bubbly. If necessary, add more cider during the baking time. The bean liquid should be very thick and juicy, but not at all dry.

6. Remove from the oven and serve.

The Michaels Family Thanksgiving Apple–Sweet Potato Bake

MAKES 6 TO 8 SERVINGS

6 medium sweet potatoes, peeled and cut crosswise into ¼-inch-thick slices

3 medium apples, peeled, cored, and cut crosswise into thin slices

1 tablespoon freshly grated orange zest

¼ cup apple cider

¼ cup pure maple syrup

2 tablespoons unsalted butter, plus more for greasing

½ teaspoon ground nutmeg

Salt and pepper, to taste

This is a traditional family side dish for almost any winter holiday or celebration. It can be made in advance and reheated just before serving.

1. Place the sweet potatoes in a large saucepan in cold water to cover by 2 inches. Place over high heat and bring to a boil. Lower the heat and cook at a gentle simmer for 25 minutes, or until just barely tender. Remove from the heat and drain well. Set aside until cool enough to handle.

2. Preheat the oven to 350°F.

3. Generously coat the interior of a 2-quart casserole with butter.

4. Place ⅓ of the sweet potatoes over the bottom of the prepared casserole. Then, cover with half of the apples. Add another layer of sweet potatoes followed by another layer of apples. Then, make a final layer of sweet potatoes. (On the final layer, you can get fancy if you would like and shingle the slices over the top like roof tiles.) Sprinkle with the orange zest. Set aside.

5. Combine the cider and maple syrup in a small saucepan over medium heat. Add the butter, nutmeg, salt, and pepper. Bring to a boil and remove from the heat. Immediately pour the mixture over the layers in the casserole.

6. Cover and place in the oven. Bake for 50 minutes; then, uncover and bake for another 10 minutes, or until the top is lightly browned and the edges are bubbly.

7. Remove from the heat and serve.

88

Cider-Glazed Carrots

MAKES 4 TO 6 SERVINGS

2 tablespoons unsalted butter

1 pound carrots, trimmed, peeled, and cut crosswise on the bias, into thin slices

1 tablespoon light brown sugar

½ cup apple cider

1 teaspoon Dijon mustard

3 tablespoons water

Salt and pepper, to taste

1. Heat the butter in a large frying pan over medium heat. Add the carrots and cook, stirring occasionally, for 3 minutes. Add the brown sugar and continue to cook, stirring, for 2 minutes, or until the sugar has dissolved.

2. Add the cider, mustard, and water and bring to a boil. Season with the salt and pepper, cover, and lower the heat. Cook, tossing occasionally to make sure the carrots are nicely glazed, for another 6 minutes, or until the carrots are crisp-tender.

3. Remove from the heat and serve.

Hot and Spicy Applesauce

MAKES ABOUT 3 CUPS

8 tart apples, peeled, cored, and cut lengthwise into quarters

4 cloves garlic, roasted

1 hot red chile, trimmed, seeded, membrane removed, and minced

½ cup low-sodium, nonfat chicken broth

2 tablespoons white wine vinegar

1 teaspoon balsamic vinegar

1 teaspoon freshly grated orange zest

½ teaspoon ground cumin

¼ teaspoon cayenne pepper *or* to taste

¼ teaspoon ground coriander

¼ cup pure maple syrup

Salt, to taste

1. Combine the apples, garlic, chile, chicken broth, vinegars, orange zest, cumin, cayenne, and coriander in a large saucepan over medium–high heat. Bring to a simmer; then, cook, stirring frequently, for 1 minute, or until the apples are mushy and the garlic can be mashed into them.

2. Add the syrup and season with the salt. Continue to cook for an additional 5 minutes, or until the flavors are blended. Taste and, if necessary, add additional cayenne, syrup, and salt.

3. Serve hot, warm, or at room temperature.

This is a terrific applesauce with roasted or grilled pork.

91

SIDES

Apples Baked in Wine

MAKES 6 SERVINGS

6 large baking apples

Juice and freshly grated zest of 1 orange

1 cup dry red wine

½ cup light brown sugar

¼ teaspoon ground nutmeg

1. Using a sharp knife, cut about 1 inch off of the stem end of each apple. Then, core straight down the middle, but not through to the blossom end. Discard the top and the core.

2. Place the apples in a slow cooker. Add the orange juice and zest along with the wine, brown sugar, and nutmeg. Cover and cook on low (200°F) for 3 hours, or until the apples are fork tender.

3. Remove from the slow cooker and serve warm or at room temperature as a side or garnish for almost any pork, sausage, or game dish.

If you don't have a slow cooker, you can either bake the apples, covered, in a Dutch oven in a very low oven (250°F) for 2 hours, or until they are very soft and fork tender. Alternately, if you want firmer apples with a glazed top, bake them, uncovered, in a baking dish for 1 hour, or until just barely cooked.

Apple–Cranberry Sauce

MAKES 1¾ POUNDS

1 pound cranberries

½ pound sweet apples, such as Gala or McIntosh, peeled, cored, and diced

½ cup light brown sugar *or* to taste

1 teaspoon freshly grated ginger

½ teaspoon ground cinnamon

Approximately ¼ cup apple cider

1. Combine the cranberries, apples, brown sugar, ginger, and cinnamon in a medium, heavy-bottomed saucepan over medium heat. Add 2 tablespoons of the cider and bring to a simmer. Cook, adding cider as necessary to keep the mixture from sticking and stirring frequently, for 20 minutes, or until the cranberries have burst and the apples are mushy. Don't add too much liquid, as you want the mixture to gel when cool.

2. Remove from the heat and scrape into a nonreactive container. Set aside to cool. Serve at room temperature, or cover and refrigerate for up to 1 week.

Hard-Cider Gravy

MAKES ABOUT 3 CUPS

Pan drippings (optional)

1 cup hard cider

3 cups low-sodium, nonfat chicken broth

4 tablespoons unsalted butter, room temperature

⅓ cup all-purpose flour

Salt and pepper, to taste

1. If using, strain pan drippings from a pot after roasting meat, poultry, or game, and strain into a clean bowl. Let stand for 10 minutes, or until the fat rises to the top. Remove and discard the fat and reserve the drippings.

2. Place the pan over medium heat and add the cider. Bring to a boil, scraping up the brown bits stuck to the bottom of the pan with a wooden spoon. Add the reserved pan drippings along with the chicken broth.

3. Place the butter in a small mixing bowl and make a roux by mashing the flour into the butter until it is a smooth paste. Whisking constantly, beat the roux into the hot cider mixture and bring to a boil.

4. Lower the heat, season with the salt and pepper and cook, whisking constantly, for 5 minutes, or until the gravy has thickened.

5. Remove from the heat and serve as is or pour through a fine mesh sieve into a gravy boat.

NOTE: *The pan drippings add deep flavor to the gravy, but are not necessary.*

94

Main
Courses

Cider Chili

1 pound dried pinto, kidney, black, or Great Northern beans

2 tablespoons canola oil

2 cups diced onions

1 tablespoon minced garlic

1½ pounds ground or chopped beef, pork, chicken, or turkey

1 (4½-ounce) can chopped green chilies

3 tablespoons chili powder

1 tablespoon ground cumin

1 teaspoon dried oregano

Salt and pepper, to taste

2 (28-ounce) cans diced tomatoes with juices

2 cups apple cider

2 tablespoons tomato paste

1. Place the beans in a large Dutch oven with cold water to cover by 2 inches. Set aside to soak for at least 8 hours or overnight. Drain well.

2. Return the soaked beans to the Dutch oven and again cover with cold water by 2 inches. Bring to a boil, lower the heat, and cook at a gentle simmer for 1½ hours, or until the beans are just barely tender. You may have to add water to keep the beans hydrated. Remove from the heat and set aside.

3. About 30 minutes before the beans are ready, prepare the chili-makings.

4. Heat the oil in a large frying pan over medium–high heat. Add the onions and garlic and cook, stirring frequently, for 5 minutes, or just until softened. Add the meat and continue to cook, stirring frequently, for 10 minutes, or until the meat has browned nicely. Stir in the chopped green chilies, chili powder, cumin, oregano, and season with the salt and pepper. Cook, stirring, for 10 minutes, or until flavors have blended. Remove from the heat.

5. When the beans are ready, add the meat mixture along with the tomatoes, cider, and tomato paste. Return to medium heat and continue to cook for another hour, or until the chili is thick and seasoned well. Taste from time to time and, if necessary, adjust the seasoning with salt, pepper, or any of the spices. If the chili gets too thick, add more cider or water, no more than ½ cup at a time.

6. Remove from the heat and serve. Store any leftovers, covered and refrigerated, for up to 3 days, or freeze for up to 3 months.

Tractor Fest Goulash

1½ tablespoons canola oil

1½ pounds beef stew meat, cut into small cubes

Salt and pepper, to taste

3 medium onions, peeled and diced

1 cup ketchup

1 cup cold water

6 tablespoons Worcestershire sauce

¼ cup light brown sugar

2 teaspoons apple cider vinegar

2 teaspoons paprika

½ teaspoon dry mustard powder

1. Heat the oil in a Dutch oven over medium heat. Season the beef with the salt and pepper and place in the hot pan. Cook, turning occasionally, for 6 minutes, or until nicely browned on all sides. This may have to be done in batches.

2. When all of the meat has been browned, add the onions and cook, stirring occasionally, for 5 minutes, or until the onions begin to take on some color. Stir in the ketchup, water, Worcestershire sauce, brown sugar, vinegar, paprika, and mustard. Cover and cook for 2 hours, or until the beef is fork tender. (If the liquid evaporates too much or becomes too thick, add up to ½ cup water. If it is too thin, combine 3 tablespoons all-purpose flour with ½ cup cold water, stirring to make a thin paste. Stir the flour paste into the goulash and cook for at least 5 minutes to eliminate the starchy taste.)

3. Remove from the heat and serve over buttered noodles, rice, or mashed potatoes, if desired.

For the tractor lover, the Fly Creek Cider Mill offers an extensive collection of vintage John Deere equipment on display and at work around the Mill. A group of single-cylinder gas engines is often operating with their interesting hit-and-miss rhythm. Children will not want to leave without exploring Tractorland (a kiddie play area with a paved little tricycle track and a wooden climb-on tractor) next to the Restaurant & Bakery.

Fly Creek Cider Beef Stew

MAKES 6 TO 8 SERVINGS

2 pounds beef stew meat, cut into large cubes

Salt and pepper, to taste

3 cups apple cider

2 tablespoons apple cider vinegar

½ teaspoon dried thyme

4 medium carrots, trimmed, peeled, and cut crosswise into ¾-inch pieces

3 medium potatoes, peeled, trimmed, and cut into large cubes

3 ribs celery, trimmed and cut crosswise into ¾-inch pieces

2 medium onions, trimmed, peeled, and cut into large wedges

¼ cup all-purpose flour

¼ cup cold water

1. Heat the oil in a Dutch oven over medium heat. Season the meat with the salt and pepper and place in the hot pan in batches, if necessary. Sear, turning occasionally, for 7 minutes, or until all sides are nicely browned. Remove the meat from the pan and drain off the fat. Carefully wipe the pan clean with a paper towel.

2. Return the meat to the pan and place over medium–high heat. Add the cider, vinegar, and thyme and bring to a boil. Lower the heat, cover, and cook at a gentle simmer for 1 hour and 15 minutes.

3. Uncover, add the carrots, potatoes, celery, and onions. Taste and, if necessary, season with the salt and pepper. Raise the heat and bring to a boil. Lower the heat, cover, and cook for 30 minutes, or until the vegetables are cooked through.

4. Combine the flour and water in a small mixing bowl, stirring to blend completely.

5. Raise the heat and, stirring constantly, add the flour mixture to the stew. Bring to a boil and boil for 2 minutes.

6. Remove from the heat and serve hot with lots of crusty bread to soak up the gravy.

> To cook in a slow cooker, dust the beef with the flour and season with salt and pepper. Place all of the vegetables in the bottom of the pot and cover with the beef. Pour in the cider and vinegar and sprinkle the thyme over the top. Cook on low for 8 to 10 hours.

The Fly Creek Cider Mill All-Time Favorite Beef Pot Roast

MAKES 6 TO 8 SERVINGS

2 tablespoons canola oil

1 (6-pound) beef rump roast

Salt and pepper, to taste (divided)

1 cup low-sodium, nonfat beef broth

1 cup cold water

½ cup dry red wine

½ cup apple cider

2 tablespoons tomato paste

2 large carrots, peeled and coarsely chopped

1 large onion, peeled and coarsely chopped

1 large tart apple, quartered

2 bay leaves

1 teaspoon dried thyme

½ teaspoon dried marjoram

1 tablespoon cornstarch (optional)

18 pearl onions, trimmed and peeled (optional)

18 baby carrots, trimmed and peeled (optional)

18 tiny new potatoes (optional)

1½ cups frozen petite peas, thawed (optional)

1. Heat the oil in a Dutch oven over medium heat. Season the roast with the salt and pepper and place it into the hot pan. Sear, turning occasionally, for 7 minutes, or until all sides are nicely browned. Remove the meat from the pan and drain off the fat. Carefully wipe the pan clean with a paper towel.

2. Return the meat to the Dutch oven over medium–high heat. Add the broth, water, wine, cider, and tomato paste, and stir to blend well. Add the carrots, onion, and apple, pushing them around in the liquid to evenly distribute. Add the bay leaves, thyme, marjoram, salt, and pepper and bring to a boil. Lower the heat to a bare simmer, cover, and cook for 2 hours, or until the meat is almost fork tender. Or, if you are not going to add the optional vegetables to the roast, continue to cook for another 30 minutes, or until the meat is fork tender.

This is one of our most requested recipes—so much so, that I keep copies on hand to share. We also serve Grandma Jane Michaels's pot roast sandwiches in our Snack Barn. They are as popular as this recipe.

3. Remove the meat from the cooking liquid and set it aside. Skim off the excess fat from the cooking liquid. Strain the liquid through a fine mesh sieve, pressing against the solids to extract as much of the liquid as possible. Discard the solids.

4. Return the meat and the strained liquid to the Dutch oven over medium heat. If not adding the optional vegetables and the gravy needs thickening, combine the cornstarch with 2 tablespoons cold water in a small mixing bowl and, stirring constantly, drizzle it into the gravy. Cook for 5 minutes to eliminate the starchy taste. Season with additional salt and pepper, if necessary.

5. Transfer the meat to a cutting board and cut into slices ¼-inch-thick. Neatly arrange on a serving platter, spoon the gravy over the top, and serve with extra gravy on the side.

6. If adding the optional vegetables, add the onions, carrots, and potatoes once the meat and strained liquid have been returned to the heat. Cook for 15 minutes, or until tender. Add the peas and cook for an additional 5 minutes.

7. If the gravy is not thick enough, remove the meat and vegetables to a serving platter and tent lightly with aluminum foil. Combine the cornstarch with 2 tablespoons cold water in a small mixing bowl and, stirring constantly, drizzle it into the gravy. Cook for 5 minutes to eliminate the starchy taste.

8. Cut the meat as directed when serving without the vegetables and serve as above.

Cider-Scented Boneless Pork Chops

MAKES 6 SERVINGS

6 (4- to 5-ounce) boneless pork chops

Salt and pepper, to taste

1 tablespoon olive oil

1 cup apple cider

⅓ cup apple jelly

½ teaspoon ground sage

1 clove garlic, peeled and mashed

2 tablespoons red wine vinegar

1. Season the pork with salt and pepper.

2. Heat the oil in a large frying pan over medium heat. When very hot, but not smoking, add the pork and fry, turning once, for 4 minutes, or until nicely browned. Remove from the pan and set aside, leaving the pan on the heat.

3. Add the cider, jelly, and sage to the hot pan. Mash the garlic into the liquid and then add the vinegar. Raise the heat and bring to a boil. Immediately lower the heat to a gentle simmer and cook, stirring occasionally, for 5 minutes, or until the liquid is reduced by half.

4. Return the chops to the pan and continue to cook, basting the chops with the sauce, for about 5 minutes, or until the chops are cooked through and nicely glazed with the sauce.

5. Remove from the pan and, using a sharp knife, cut on the bias into thin slices. Place on a serving platter and drizzle the pan sauce over the top.

6. Serve immediately.

Grilled Marinated Hanger Steak

MAKES 4 TO 6 SERVINGS

2 (1½-pound) hanger steaks, trimmed of membrane and cut in half lengthwise

1 cup Fly Creek Cider Mill Zinfandel Tri-Tip Grill Marinade, plus more for brushing *or* your favorite steak marinade or grilling sauce (divided)

Salt and pepper, to taste

1. Place the steaks in a large, shallow bowl. Add 1 cup of the marinade and toss to coat well. Cover with plastic film and set aside to marinate for 30 minutes at room temperature or up to 2 hours in the refrigerator.

2. If the steak has been refrigerated, remove it from the refrigerator 30 minutes before you are ready to grill and let it come to room temperature.

3. When ready to grill, preheat and oil the grill. Alternately, preheat and oil a stove-top grill pan and grill as directed.

4. Season the steaks with the salt and pepper and place on the hottest part of the grill. Using a pastry brush, lightly brush the steaks with marinade and grill for 1 minute or just until the first side is marked. Turn and lightly brush the other side with marinade and grill for an additional minute to mark.

5. Move the steaks to a slightly cooler part of the grill and continue to grill, turning and brushing with marinade occasionally, for 8 minutes, or until an instant-read thermometer registers 150°F when inserted into the thickest part. Once rested, this should give you a medium-rare steak (see sidebar).

6. Remove from the grill and transfer to a cutting board to rest for 5 minutes before cutting, crosswise, into thin slices.

7. Place the slices on a platter and serve immediately.

We sell quite a few sauces and marinades, but this particular one tops the Michaels family list. It is named for Brenda's brother, Chef Charlie Palmer, who is a big proponent of tri-tip steak and zinfandel wines, both California favorites. Like tri-tip steak, hanger steak is very flavorful, low in fat, and usually less expensive that most other steaks. However, because of its low fat content, hanger steak should only be grilled to medium-rare, as it tends to dry out otherwise.

105

Pork Braised in Hard Cider

MAKES 6 SERVINGS

1 tablespoon canola oil

1 (5-pound) pork butt

Salt and pepper, to taste

2 onions, peeled and sliced

2 carrots, peeled and cut into large pieces

1½ cups cherry tomatoes

4 sprigs parsley

3 cloves garlic, peeled and minced

Sachet (1 teaspoon each celery seed, mustard seed, whole allspice tied in a cheesecloth bag)

Freshly grated zest of ½ orange

3½ cups hard cider

2 cups low-sodium, nonfat chicken broth

1 tablespoon cornstarch

2 tablespoons water

1. Heat the oil in a large Dutch oven over medium heat. Season the pork with the salt and pepper and add it to the pan. Sear, turning frequently, for 10 minutes, or until browned on all sides. Remove the meat from the pan and set aside, and pour off all but 1 tablespoon of the fat, leaving the browned bits in the bottom of the pan.

2. Return the pan to medium heat and add the onions, carrots, and tomatoes, stirring to coat with the fat. Cook, stirring frequently, for 4 minutes. Add the parsley, garlic, sachet, and orange zest, stirring to combine.

3. Return the meat to the pan. Add the hard cider and chicken broth, cover, and bring to a simmer.

4. Lower the heat and simmer for 2 hours. Uncover and continue to simmer for another hour, or until the meat is just about falling apart.

5. Lift the meat from the liquid and set aside.

6. Strain the cooking liquid through a fine mesh sieve, discarding the solids. Return the strained liquid to the pan.

7. Mix the cornstarch and water, stirring to dissolve. Whisk the cornstarch mixture into the liquid. Return the pot to medium heat and, stirring frequently, bring to a simmer. Lower the heat and simmer for 5 minutes, or until the starchy taste has cooked out and the sauce is thick and shiny. Taste and, if necessary, season with the salt and pepper.

This is the Fly Creek Cider Mill version of pulled pork. Not only does the pork make a terrific dinner with noodles, the meat makes a great sandwich piled high with pickles and coleslaw. If you're lucky, you'll have leftovers and can experience both.

8. While the sauce is cooking, pull the meat apart, discarding the fat.

9. When ready to serve, place the meat in a frying pan and ladle the sauce over the top. Place over medium heat and cook to just heat through.

10. Remove from the heat and serve.

Roast Loin of Pork
with Apple Cider–Mustard Sauce

MAKES 4 SERVINGS

¼ cup granulated sugar

3 tablespoons coarse salt, plus more, to taste

1 (2½–3-pound) boneless pork loin, most of the fat removed

Freshly ground pepper, to taste

1¼ cups apple cider (divided)

1 cup water

4 tablespoons unsalted butter

⅓ cup chopped shallots

¼ teaspoon minced hot green chile *or* to taste

4 tart apples, peeled, cored, and chopped

1½ cups heavy cream

1 tablespoon Dijon mustard

1 tablespoon honey mustard

Fresh juice of ½ lime

1 tablespoon chopped flat-leaf parsley

1. Combine the sugar and 3 tablespoons of the salt in a large resealable plastic bag. Add the pork, seal, and shake to help dissolve the sugar and salt. Refrigerate for 1 to 3 hours.

2. When ready to roast, preheat the oven to 450°F.

3. Remove the pork from the refrigerator and pour off and discard the brine. Pat the meat dry.

4. Season the pork with additional salt and pepper and place it on a rack set in a roasting pan. Add 1 cup of the cider and the water.

5. Place in the oven and roast, basting occasionally, for 1½ hours, or until an instant-read thermometer inserted into the thickest part reads 160°F.

6. While the pork is roasting, make the sauce.

7. Heat the butter in a heavy-bottomed saucepan over medium heat. Add the shallots and chile and sauté for 5 minutes, or until the shallots are very soft. Add the apples along with the remaining ¼ cup of cider, stirring to blend. Lower the heat, cover, and cook for 10 minutes, or just until the apples have softened. Stir in the cream and mustards; season with the salt and pepper. Cook, stirring frequently, for 10 minutes, or until the apples are mushy and the liquid has thickened slightly.

8. Remove from the heat and transfer to a blender (this may have to be done in batches) and process to a smooth purée.

9. Pour the purée through a fine mesh sieve into a clean saucepan. Add the lime juice, stirring to blend. Taste and, if necessary, add additional salt and pepper. Keep warm until ready to serve.

10. Remove the pork from the oven and let rest for at least 5 minutes before slicing.

11. Using a sharp chef's knife, cut the pork, crosswise, into slices. Place the slices down the center of a serving platter. Spoon the warm sauce over the top, sprinkle with the parsley, and serve immediately.

Barbecued Spareribs

MAKES 6 SERVINGS

1 (5-pound) slab spareribs *or* baby back ribs

¾ cup Fly Creek Cider Mill Squealin' Pork Spice Rub *or* spice rub of your choice

1½ cups Fly Creek Cider Mill 1856 Barbecue Sauce (see page 28) *or* barbecue sauce of your choice

1. Preheat the oven to 325°F.

2. Place a wire rack on a baking sheet with sides. Set aside.

3. Generously coat both sides of the ribs with the spice rub, using your hands to make sure that the rub adheres to the meat. Then, lay the seasoned ribs on a sheet of heavy-duty aluminum foil large enough to completely enclose them. Tightly wrap, taking care that the seam is sealed. (This can be done up to 2 days in advance to allow the seasoning to penetrate the meat. If so, refrigerate the ribs until 30 minutes before ready to cook.)

4. Place the wrapped ribs on the wire rack and place on the middle rack in the oven. Bake for 2 hours for spareribs or 90 minutes for baby back ribs.

5. About 30 minutes before the ribs are done, remove them from the oven and unwrap. Using a pastry brush, lightly coat each side with the barbecue sauce. Return coated ribs to the wire rack and place back in the oven. After 15 minutes, brush again with barbecue sauce. The ribs should be slightly charred, and the meat should be easily pierced with the tip of a sharp knife, but not falling off of the bone.

6. Remove from the oven and let rest for 5 minutes. Then, using a sharp knife, cut the ribs between the bones to make individual ribs.

7. Serve immediately with barbecue sauce on the side.

These ribs can be made on the barbecue, but we like this recipe because it lets us enjoy barbecue all year long. If you decide to put them on the grill, follow the same procedure, but do the initial cooking on the cooler side of the grill.

Smoked Pork Sausage with Hard-Cider Sauce

MAKES 6 SERVINGS

2 teaspoons canola oil

½ pound smoked thick-sliced bacon, cut into pieces

1 large onion, peeled and chopped

1½–2 pounds smoked pork *or* chicken sausage

1 tablespoon all-purpose flour

2 cups hard apple cider

2 cloves garlic, peeled and smashed

1 bay leaf

½ teaspoon ground dried sage

Salt and pepper, to taste

2 tablespoons unsalted butter

1 large apple, cored, and cut crosswise into slices ⅛-inch thick (leave unpeeled)

1. Preheat the oven to 350°F.

2. Heat the oil in a Dutch oven over medium heat. Add the bacon and onion and cook, stirring frequently, for 5 minutes, or until the bacon begins to color. Add the sausage and continue to cook, turning occasionally, for 10 minutes, or until the bacon has crisped and the sausage is brown. If the sausage has exuded too much fat, use a double layer of paper towel to absorb some of it.

3. Sprinkle the flour over the pan juices and stir to blend well. When blended, add the cider, stirring to incorporate the flour into the liquid. Add the garlic, bay leaf, sage, salt, and pepper. Bring to a simmer, cover, and place in the oven.

4. Bake for 30 minutes, then uncover and cook for an additional 10 minutes, or until the sausage is thoroughly cooked and the sauce has thickened.

5. While the sausage is braising, prepare the apples.

6. Melt the butter in a large frying pan over medium heat. Add the apples and cook, gently tossing and turning with tongs, for 5 minutes, or until the apples are golden brown. Watch carefully as you don't want them to be mushy. Remove from the heat and set aside. The apples don't need to be piping hot for serving.

7. When the sausage is done, place it along with the pan gravy on a serving platter. Remove the bay leaf, garnish with the apples, and serve immediately.

Apple-Scented Roast Chicken

MAKES 4 TO 6 SERVINGS

4 cups apple juice

4 cups cold water

1 cinnamon stick

¼ cup salt, plus more, to taste

¼ cup granulated sugar

1 tablespoon black peppercorns

1 (3½–4 pound) roasting chicken

1 lemon

Freshly ground black pepper, to taste

1 medium apple (optional)

1 cup apple cider

1 cup low-sodium chicken broth

There are more chickens in the world than any other domesticated bird— more than one chicken for every human being!

1. Combine the apple juice and water in a 2-gallon resealable plastic bag. Add the cinnamon stick along with the salt, sugar, and peppercorns. Seal and let rest for 30 minutes, or until the salt and sugar have dissolved.

2. Unseal and place the chicken into the brine. Seal and refrigerate for 1 to 8 hours.

3. Remove the chicken from the refrigerator and drain it well. Rinse under cold, running water and pat dry. Set aside for 20 minutes while it reaches room temperature.

4. Preheat the oven to 450°F.

5. Cut a lemon in half and rub the skin of the chicken with the cut side of the lemon, making sure that the juice really coats the skin. Season both the skin and the cavity with the salt and pepper. If using, insert the apple into the cavity and truss the cavity closed. The apple will add additional flavor to the roasted meat. Fold the wings under the back and tie the legs together using kitchen twine.

6. Place the chicken on a rack in a roasting pan. Add the cider and chicken broth and place in the hot oven. Roast for 30 minutes; then reduce the temperature to 350°F and continue to roast for an additional 30 minutes, or until the skin is golden brown and crisp and an instant-read thermometer inserted into the thickest part reads 160°F. The USDA gives 165°F as the proper internal temperature, but if you roast to 160°F and then let the chicken rest for 10 minutes before carving, the internal temperate will rise and the meat will be thoroughly cooked without being overcooked.

7. Remove from the oven and let rest for 10 to 15 minutes before carving.

Cider-Braised Chicken

MAKES 4 TO 6 SERVINGS

1 (4-pound) chicken, cut into serving pieces

Salt and white pepper, to taste

3 tablespoons olive oil

1 cup apple cider

⅓ cup dry white wine

1 cup heavy cream

1 teaspoon chopped fresh sage

1 teaspoon fresh thyme leaves

1. Preheat the oven to 400°F.

2. Rinse and dry the chicken. Season with the salt and pepper.

3. Heat the oil in a Dutch oven over medium heat. When very hot, but not smoking, add the chicken. Brown, turning frequently, for 10 minutes, or until the chicken is nicely colored.

4. Using tongs, remove the chicken to a double layer of paper towel to quickly absorb any excess fat. Then, transfer to a plate.

5. Discard any of the remaining oil in the pan.

6. Return the pan to medium heat. Add the cider and wine and bring to a boil. Lower the heat and stir in the cream, sage, and thyme. Bring to a simmer.

7. Return the chicken, along with any juices on the plate, to the pan, spooning the sauce over the top of each piece. Cover and place in the oven.

8. Braise for 25 minutes, or until the chicken is cooked through and the sauce has thickened.

9. Remove from the oven and transfer the chicken to a serving platter. Taste the sauce and, if necessary, season with additional salt and pepper. (If the sauce has separated and is not thick enough to serve as gravy, place the pan over medium heat. Bring to a simmer, whisking constantly to blend and thicken the sauce.) Spoon the sauce over the top and serve with rice, noodles, or mashed potatoes.

Apple–Swiss Chicken and Ham Rolls

MAKES 6 SERVINGS

6 thin chicken cutlets

1½ teaspoons Italian seasoning

Salt and pepper, to taste

6 thin slices smoked ham

1 tart apple, peeled, cored, halved, and cut lengthwise into thin slices

1 tablespoon olive oil

6 thin slices Swiss cheese

¼ cup apple cider

Paprika, for sprinkling

1. Generously butter the interior of a 2-quart baking dish. Set aside.

2. Preheat oven to 350°F.

3. Lay the cutlets out on a clean, flat work surface. Season 1 side of each cutlet with the Italian seasoning, salt, and pepper. Lay a slice of ham on the seasoned side of each cutlet; then, lay a few slices of apple on top of the ham. Using your fingertips, roll each cutlet up, cigar-fashion, and secure the seal by threading a toothpick through the seam.

4. Place the chicken rolls in a single layer in the prepared baking dish. Drizzle a bit of oil over each one and then wrap a piece of cheese around them. Drizzle the cider over the rolls and sprinkle with paprika.

5. Place in the oven and bake for 15 minutes, or until the chicken is cooked through and the cheese has melted.

6. Remove from the oven, remove toothpicks, and transfer the chicken rolls to a serving platter. Serve hot.

NOTE: *Make sure you don't add too much salt to the chicken cutlets— the ham will add some saltiness.*

Cider-Basted Turkey

MAKES 6 TO 8 SERVINGS

1 (12- to 14-pound) turkey

Salt and pepper, to taste

3 shallots, peeled and halved

1 tart apple, such as Crispin, peeled, cored, and quartered

1 large sprig flat-leaf parsley

1 teaspoon dried sage

4 tablespoons unsalted butter, room temperature

1 cup hard cider

1 cup Fly Creek Cider Mill Apple Wine *or* other dry white wine

½ cup apple brandy

4 large baking apples, peeled, cored, and cut lengthwise in half

1½ cups low-sodium turkey broth

2 tablespoons cornstarch dissolved in 2 tablespoons cold water

1. Preheat the oven to 425°F.

2. Season the cavity of the turkey with the salt and pepper. Place the shallots, apple, parsley, and sage into the cavity. Truss the cavity closed.

3. Fold the wings under the back and tie the legs together using kitchen twine. Place the turkey on a wire rack in a roasting pan. Using your fingertips, rub the entire exterior with the butter; season with the salt and pepper.

4. Combine the hard cider, wine, and brandy. Pour 1 cup of the mixture into the roasting pan and set the rest aside. Loosely cover the turkey with heavy-duty aluminum foil, taking care that it does not stick to the skin.

5. Place in the oven and roast for 1 hour, basting frequently with the remaining cider mixture. When the cider mixture has been used, baste with the pan juices. Uncover, lower the oven temperature to 325°F, and continue to roast for 30 minutes.

6. Randomly place the apple halves around the turkey. Baste the apples with the pan juices and continue to roast, basting frequently, for another 30 minutes, or until an instant-read thermometer registers 165°F and the apples are cooked through but holding their shape.

7. Remove from the oven and transfer the turkey to a serving platter. Surround the turkey with the roasted apple halves and lightly tent with aluminum foil to keep warm.

8. Pour the pan juices into a large measuring cup (or into a fat separator) and let rest for a few minutes, allowing the fat to rise to the top. Skim off and discard the fat.

9. Return the pan juices to the roasting pan (or other stovetop-safe pan) and place it over medium heat on the stovetop. Add the turkey broth and whisk to combine. Whisking constantly, pour the cornstarch mixture into the pan. Cook, stirring constantly, for 7 minutes, or until the gravy has thickened and the starchy taste has cooked out. Taste and then season with additional salt and pepper, if necessary. Remove from the heat and pour into a gravy boat.

10. Present the turkey at the table and then carve and serve with the apples and gravy.

This is the most perfect Thanksgiving turkey recipe as it brings the flavors of fall to the pan. The cooking aromas of hard cider, apple wine, and apple brandy wafting over the holiday smells of roasting turkey will fill your house with the scents of celebration. In our area, many folks use wild turkey for this recipe.

Fish and Chips

MAKES 6 SERVINGS

1½ cups all-purpose flour

¼ cup baking powder

1¾ cups sparkling cider, beer, or seltzer (see note)

Approximately 2 quarts vegetable oil, for frying

1½ pounds thin white fish fillets

Salt and pepper, to taste

½ cup Wondra flour (see note)

Chips (French Fries) (recipe follows)

Apple cider vinegar, for splashing on the fish and chips

1. Preheat the oven to 250°F and set aside a baking sheet.

2. Combine the flour and baking powder in a medium mixing bowl. Whisk in the cider, beer, or seltzer. The batter should be as thick as heavy cream. Set aside.

3. Place the oil in a deep fat fryer or large frying pan over medium–high heat. Bring to 360°F on an instant-read thermometer.

4. Pat each fillet dry and season with the salt and pepper. Dust both sides of each fillet with Wondra flour. Then, working with 1 piece at a time, dip the fillets into the batter, allowing excess to drip off.

5. Again, working with 1 piece at a time and holding one end, gently lower the coated fillets into the hot oil. Fry for 4 minutes, or until the exterior is golden brown and crisp. Do not crowd the pan; fry in batches, if necessary.

6. As the fish pieces are fried, place them on a double layer of paper towel to drain off excess oil. Season with the salt. Transfer the fried fish to the baking sheet. Place in the oven, leaving the door ajar so the fish does not continue to cook.

7. Prepare the Chips (French Fries) according to the recipe that follows.

8. Combine with the chips in a cone made of newspaper. Serve hot with vinegar for seasoning both the fish and the chips.

NOTE: *The cider will add a sweet note, the beer a hint of malt, and the seltzer just the bubbles.*

Wondra flour is a very fine flour that is sold in most supermarkets. It lightly coats as well as creates a smooth gravy.

119

CHIPS (FRENCH FRIES)

MAKES 6 SERVINGS

6 medium Idaho or russet potatoes, peeled and cut lengthwise into ¼-inch strips

Approximately 2 quarts vegetable oil, for frying

Salt, to taste

1. Place sliced potatoes in a large mixing bowl and cover with cold water by 2 inches. Let stand for 15 minutes.

2. Place the oil in a deep fat fryer or large frying pan over medium-high heat. Bring to 350°F on an instant-read thermometer.

3. Drain the potatoes well and pat dry with a clean kitchen towel. They should be very dry.

4. Carefully drop the potatoes into the hot oil, a large handful at a time. You don't want to crowd the pan as it will lower the oil temperature too much and the potatoes will get soggy as they fry. Fry, turning occasionally, for 6 minutes, or until just barely colored.

5. Remove the potatoes from the oil and transfer to a triple layer of paper towel to drain. When all of the potatoes have been fried for the first time, raise the temperature of the oil to 375°. Add the potatoes, again in batches, and fry for a second time for 2 minutes, or until golden brown and crisp.

6. Remove from the oil and place in a brown paper bag. Season with the salt and shake to remove excess oil.

7. Serve hot, drizzled with vinegar or ketchup.

If you want to take a major shortcut, you can always use frozen breaded fish fillets and french fries and cook according to the manufacturer's directions. The key to the classic dish is serving the fish and chips in a newspaper cone along with either cider or malt vinegar.

Apple Butter–Glazed Salmon

MAKES 6 SERVINGS

½ cup Apple Butter (see page 33) *or* other fine quality apple butter

2 tablespoons Dijon mustard

6 (6-ounce) salmon fillets

2 tablespoons unsalted butter, melted

Salt and pepper, to taste

1. Preheat the oven to 425°F.

2. Combine the apple butter and mustard in a small mixing bowl. Set aside.

3. Place the salmon fillets on a baking sheet lined with nonstick aluminum foil. Using a pastry brush, lightly coat the salmon with the melted butter, salt, and pepper. Place in the oven and bake for 10 minutes.

4. Remove the salmon from the oven and raise the oven temperature to broil.

5. Using a pastry brush, generously coat the top of each piece of salmon with the apple butter mixture.

6. Place under the broiler and broil for 2 minutes, or until the top is glazed and the salmon flakes easily when poked with the tip of a small sharp knife.

7. Remove from the broiler and serve hot or at room temperature.

Trout with Apples and Dill

MAKES 6 SERVINGS

6 (12-ounce) trout, scaled, cleaned, and heads removed

Salt and pepper, to taste

1 cup finely diced tart apple

2 tablespoons chopped fresh dill

1 tablespoon Fly Creek Cider Mill Old English Horseradish Sauce *or* other fine quality bottled horseradish sauce *or* plain horseradish

Freshly grated zest of 1 lemon

3 tablespoons unsalted butter, melted

Fresh dill sprigs, for garnish (optional)

Lemon wedges, for garnish (optional)

1. Preheat the oven to 400°F.

2. Line a large baking sheet with sides with nonstick aluminum foil. Set aside.

3. Rinse each trout under cold running water and pat dry. Season the cavity with the salt and pepper.

4. Combine the apple, dill, horseradish, and lemon zest in a small mixing bowl. When blended, spoon an equal portion into the cavity of each trout, taking care to pull the top over the stuffing. Place the stuffed trout on the prepared baking sheet.

5. Using a pastry brush, lightly coat each trout with the butter, then season with the salt and pepper.

6. Wrap the entire pan in nonstick aluminum foil and place in the oven. Bake for 10 minutes, or until the fish is just cooked through. Uncover and bake for another 4 minutes, or until lightly colored.

7. Remove from the oven and serve hot, garnished with the fresh dill sprigs and lemon wedges, if using.

Halibut with Apple and Fennel

MAKES 6 SERVINGS

1 medium onion, peeled and minced

½ cup peeled, minced tart apple

½ cup minced fennel

3 tablespoons Dijon mustard

3 tablespoons peanut oil (divided)

6 (6-ounce) halibut fillets

Salt and pepper, to taste

4 tablespoons unsalted butter (divided)

¼ cup white balsamic vinegar

1. Combine the onion, apple, fennel, mustard, and 2 tablespoons of the oil in a medium mixing bowl. Using your hands, evenly coat both sides of the fish with the onion mixture and place the fish in a glass baking dish. When all of the fish have been coated and placed in the dish, cover the dish with plastic film. Transfer to the refrigerator to marinate for 4 to 8 hours.

2. About 30 minutes before you are ready to cook, remove the fish from the refrigerator and let stand for 15 minutes.

3. Unwrap the fish and season with the salt and pepper.

4. Combine 1 tablespoon of the butter and the remaining 1 tablespoon of oil in a large frying pan over medium–high heat. Add the fish and cook for 4 minutes, or until the bottoms are brown and slightly crisp. Using a fish spatula (or other large spatula), carefully turn each fillet and cook for 5 minutes, or until the remaining side is brown and crisp and the fish is just barely cooked through. Using the spatula, transfer the fish to a serving platter, leaving the pan on the heat.

5. Add the vinegar to the frying pan, using a wooden spoon to scrape up any browned bits from the bottom of the pan. Stir in the remaining 3 tablespoons of butter and cook, stirring constantly, for 30 seconds, or until a thin sauce has formed. Pour the sauce over the halibut and serve immediately.

Oven-Barbecued Shrimp

MAKES 6 SERVINGS

2 pounds large shrimp, shells on, split open down the center of back

1¼ cups Fly Creek Cider Mill 1856 Barbecue Sauce (see page 28) *or* your favorite barbecue sauce, plus more for dipping

1. Combine the shrimp with the barbecue sauce in a shallow baking dish, tossing to cover completely. Cover with plastic film and refrigerate for 3 hours.

2. Preheat the oven to 350°F.

3. Remove the shrimp from the refrigerator and unwrap. Place in the oven and bake for 12 minutes, or until the shrimp is completely cooked and starting to crisp on the edges.

4. Remove from the oven and serve with extra barbecue sauce on the side for dipping.

NOTE: *You can also place the shrimp on skewers and grill.*

Rabbit with Apples and Mustard

MAKES 6 TO 8 SERVINGS

2 (2½- to 3-pound) rabbits, each cut into 6 pieces (2 front legs, 2 back legs, and the loin cut into 2 pieces), plus the ribs and the flap meat

1 cup all-purpose flour

Salt and pepper, to taste

¼ cup olive oil

4 tablespoons unsalted butter

6 large shallots, trimmed and peeled

1 knob celery root, peeled, cleaned, and cut into large cubes

3 tart apples, peeled, cored, and cut into large cubes

2 cups apple cider

1 cup low-sodium, nonfat chicken broth

¼ cup grainy mustard

1 tablespoon Dijon mustard

1 tablespoon light brown sugar

1 tablespoon chopped fresh thyme

1. Place the rabbit pieces in a 2-gallon resealable plastic bag. Add the flour, salt, and pepper. Seal and shake to coat the rabbit in the seasoned flour. Set aside.

2. Heat the oil and butter in a Dutch oven over medium heat. Add the seasoned rabbit, in batches if necessary, and sear, turning frequently, until nicely browned. When browned, using tongs, transfer the rabbit to a double layer of paper towel to allow excess fat to drain off.

3. Drain half of the fat from the pan and return it to medium heat. Add the shallots and celery root and cook, stirring frequently, for 5 minutes, or until lightly colored.

4. Return the rabbit to the pan along with the apples, tossing to blend into the vegetables.

5. Combine the cider, broth, mustards, brown sugar, and thyme in a small mixing bowl and pour over the rabbit. Cover and bring to a simmer. Cook at a gentle simmer for 45 minutes, or until the rabbit is tender and the sauce has thickened slightly.

6. Remove from the heat and serve with mashed potatoes, rice, or buttered noodles, if desired.

All through Upstate New York many, many people raise rabbits for food. They are lean with white meat and should be braised, as in this recipe, until the meat is almost falling off the bone. They are usually inexpensive and are often fried in place of chicken.

Venison Stew

MAKES 6 TO 8 SERVINGS

2 pounds venison stew meat, cut into cubes

½ cup all-purpose flour

½ teaspoon dried thyme

½ teaspoon dried sage

½ teaspoon dried marjoram

Salt and pepper, to taste

5 medium carrots, trimmed, peeled, and cut crosswise into ¾-inch pieces

5 medium potatoes, peeled and cut into large cubes

3 turnips, trimmed, peeled, and cut into cubes

2 tart apples, peeled, cored, and cut into cubes

1 onion, trimmed, peeled, and diced

2½ cups apple cider

1. Place the venison in a large mixing bowl. Combine the flour, thyme, sage, marjoram, salt, and pepper and sprinkle it over the meat, tossing to coat well.

2. Place the carrots, potatoes, turnips, apples, and onion in the bottom of a slow cooker. Lay the seasoned meat over the top, sprinkling any remaining flour mixture over it.

3. Pour the cider over the top, cover, and cook on low for 10 to 12 hours.

4. Serve hot with Cornbread with Bacon, Apples, and Onion (see page 137) or other cornbread.

> In our area, we have many, many hunters and an overabundance of deer and wild turkey. Customers are always asking for venison recipes, and this one is a favorite in the fall.

Apple–Cheddar Quiche

MAKES 1 9-INCH QUICHE OR 6 INDIVIDUAL QUICHES

2 large tart apples, peeled, cored, and cut lengthwise into thin slices

3 tablespoons apple cider

3 large eggs, room temperature

1 cup cottage cheese

1 cup shredded extra-sharp Cheddar cheese

¼ cup whole milk

⅛ teaspoon ground nutmeg

Salt and pepper, to taste

1 9-inch tart pan lined with Mill-Aged Cheddar Pie Pastry (see page 37) *or* 6 4-inch tart pans lined with pastry (see note)

1. Preheat the oven to 325°F.

2. Place the apple slices in a large frying pan with the cider. Bring to a simmer and immediately remove from the heat and let rest for 5 minutes. Using a slotted spoon, transfer the apples to a double layer of paper towel to drain well.

3. Combine the eggs with the cottage cheese and Cheddar cheese in a blender jar. Add the milk and season with the nutmeg, salt, and pepper. Process until smooth.

4. Place the drained apples in the bottom of the pastry-lined pie pan. Or, if making individual quiches, place an equal number of the apple slices over the bottom of each pastry-lined pan. Carefully pour the cheese mixture over the top, keeping the apples in an even layer over the bottom.

5. Place in the oven and bake for 50 minutes, or until the point of a small, sharp knife inserted in the center comes out clean.

6. Remove from the oven and place on a wire rack for 10 minutes before cutting and serving.

NOTE: *If you don't have time to make the pastry, a refrigerated pie crust will work just fine. Or, you can bake the cheese mixture in a well-buttered deep-dish pie plate if you want to eliminate the crust altogether.*

129

Hard Cider Mac 'n' Cheese

MAKES 6 SERVINGS

1 (13½-ounce) box macaroni

3 tablespoons unsalted butter, plus more for greasing

1 tart apple, peeled, cored, and finely diced

1 small yellow onion, trimmed, peeled, and finely diced

3 tablespoons whole-wheat flour

1 cup hard cider

1 cup heavy cream

Salt and pepper, to taste

1½ pounds grated fine quality Cheddar cheese

1. Preheat the oven to 350°F.

2. Generously butter the interior of a 2-quart baking dish or casserole. Set aside.

3. Cook the macaroni according to the manufacturer's directions. Drain and pour into the prepared baking dish.

4. Melt the butter in a medium saucepan over medium–low heat. Add the apple and onion and cook, stirring frequently, for 7 minutes, or until the apple and onion have softened and exuded some liquid.

5. Sprinkle the flour over the mixture, stirring to evenly coat. When the flour has been absorbed by the liquid and no lumps appear, slowly pour in the cider, whisking constantly, followed by the cream. Raise the heat and bring to a boil.

6. When boiling, add approximately ¾ of the cheese, stirring constantly until it has melted into the sauce. Immediately pour the sauce over the macaroni, stirring to blend. Taste and, if necessary, season with the salt and pepper.

7. Sprinkle the remaining cheese over the top and place in the oven. Bake for 20 minutes, or until the edges are bubbling and the top is golden brown.

8. Remove from the heat and serve immediately.

Pumpkin Lasagna

MAKES 10 TO 12 SERVINGS

2 (15-ounce) cans pumpkin

2 tablespoons extra virgin olive oil, plus more for greasing

1 tablespoon unsalted butter

1 cup finely chopped onion

1 teaspoon minced garlic

1 teaspoon minced fresh sage *or* ½ teaspoon dried

½ cup nonfat milk

¼ cup hard cider

1 teaspoon apple cider vinegar

Salt and pepper, to taste

12 no-cook lasagna noodles

1 (15-ounce) container ricotta cheese

1 pound fresh mozzarella cheese, cut into thin slices

½ cup shredded Cheddar cheese

¼ cup grated Parmesan cheese

1. Place the pumpkin in a fine mesh sieve set over a bowl and let drain for 90 minutes to eliminate some of the liquid.

2. Preheat the oven to 400°F.

3. Lightly coat the interior of a 3-quart, preferably oval, baking dish with olive oil. Set aside.

4. Combine the olive oil and butter in a large saucepan over medium heat. Add the onion, garlic, and sage. Cook, stirring frequently, for 5 minutes, or until just softened. Stir in the drained pumpkin, milk, cider, and vinegar. Season with the salt and pepper and cook, stirring frequently, for 7 minutes, or until very hot. Remove from the heat.

5. Spoon an even layer of the pumpkin mixture over the bottom of the prepared baking dish. Cover with 4 of the noodles. Spoon about ⅓ of the remaining sauce over the noodles. Top with a layer of the ricotta, followed by a layer of the mozzarella, and finally a sprinkle of the Cheddar. Repeat to make 2 additional layers, ending with a layer of Cheddar.

6. Place in the oven and bake for 40 minutes. Sprinkle with the Parmesan cheese and return to the oven for an additional 5 to 10 minutes, or until the lasagna is bubbling and the top is golden.

7. Remove from the oven and transfer to a wire rack. Allow to rest for 15 minutes before cutting and serving.

Black Bean and Apple Stew

MAKES 6 SERVINGS

2 tablespoons extra virgin olive oil

3 cloves garlic, peeled and minced

1 large carrot, trimmed, peeled, and finely diced

1 medium onion, trimmed, peeled, and finely diced

1 teaspoon freshly grated ginger

Freshly grated zest of 1 lemon

3 cups cooked black beans

1 (15-ounce) can diced tomatoes with their juice

3 cups low-sodium, nonfat chicken broth *or* vegetable broth

1 tablespoon curry powder

1 teaspoon ground cumin

¼ teaspoon cayenne pepper *or* to taste

Salt and pepper, to taste

2 cups (about 3 large) diced parsnips

1½ cups diced tart apple

1 cup chopped button mushrooms

2 cups chopped kale

1. Heat the oil in a Dutch oven over medium heat. Add the garlic, carrot, and onion and cook, stirring frequently, for 5 minutes, or just until the carrot is beginning to soften. Stir in the ginger and lemon zest and cook for another minute.

2. Add the black beans along with the tomatoes and broth. Season with the curry, cumin, cayenne, salt and pepper and bring to a boil. Lower the heat, cover, and cook for 15 minutes.

3. Add the parsnips, apples, and mushrooms, stirring to blend. Cover and continue to cook for another 15 minutes. Stir in the kale and continue to cook for another 5 minutes, or until the black beans are almost mushy and the vegetables are tender.

4. Remove from the heat and serve with Fly Creek Cider Biscuits (see page 146), if desired.

133

Baked Squash with Apple–Quinoa Stuffing

MAKES 6 SERVINGS

3 delicata *or* small acorn squash, cut in half lengthwise and seeded

3 tablespoons olive oil (divided)

Salt and pepper, to taste (divided)

2 tablespoons unsalted butter

1 medium onion, trimmed, peeled, and finely diced

1 small carrot, trimmed, peeled, and finely diced

1 clove garlic, peeled and minced

3 cups cooked quinoa

1 large tart apple, peeled, cored, and finely diced

½ cup golden raisins

¼ cup toasted pine nuts

1 tablespoon chopped flat-leaf parsley

About ½ cup apple cider

1 cup shredded fine quality Cheddar cheese

1. Preheat the oven to 350°F.

2. Line a baking sheet with nonstick aluminum foil.

3. Lightly coat the cavity and the cut side of each squash half using half of the oil. Season with the salt and pepper and place, cut side down, on the prepared baking sheet. Place in the oven and bake for 1 hour, or until almost cooked through.

4. While the squash is baking, prepare the stuffing.

5. Heat the remaining oil along with the butter in a large frying pan over medium heat. Add the onion, carrot, and garlic and cook, stirring, for 6 minutes, or until slightly tender. Add the quinoa along with the apple, raisins, pine nuts, and parsley, stirring to blend. Season with the salt and pepper and continue to cook, stirring occasionally, for 10 minutes, or until the flavors have blended. Add just enough of the cider to moisten. Remove from the heat.

6. Remove the squash from the oven and leave the oven on.

7. Leaving the squash on the baking sheet, turn each half cut-side-up. Generously stuff the cavity of each half with an equal portion of the stuffing, mounding slightly in the center. Sprinkle an equal portion of the cheese over each one and return to the oven.

8. Bake for 15 minutes, or until the squash is cooked through, the stuffing is hot, and the cheese has melted and taken on a little color.

9. Remove from the oven and serve immediately.

135

Breads

Cornbread with Bacon, Apples, and Onion

MAKES 6 TO 8 SERVINGS

1 tablespoon olive oil

½ pound smoked thick-sliced bacon, cut into small pieces

1 cup diced sweet onion

2 medium sweet apples, peeled, cored, and cut lengthwise into thin slices

2 tablespoons light brown sugar

1½ cups cornmeal

1 cup all-purpose flour

¼ cup granulated sugar

1 tablespoon baking powder

½ teaspoon baking soda

½ teaspoon salt

2 large eggs, beaten, room temperature

1½ cups buttermilk, room temperature

7 tablespoons unsalted butter, melted (divided)

1. Preheat the oven to 400°F.

2. Heat the oil in a medium frying pan over medium heat. Add the bacon and onion and cook, stirring occasionally, for 7 minutes, or until the bacon has crisped and the onion is golden brown.

3. Stir in the apples and brown sugar. Continue to cook for another 4 minutes, or until the apples have begun to color. Remove from the heat and set aside.

4. Combine the cornmeal, flour, sugar, baking powder, baking soda, and salt in a medium mixing bowl. Set aside.

5. Combine the eggs and buttermilk with 4 tablespoons of the melted butter in a small mixing bowl, whisking to blend. Pour the egg mixture into the dry ingredients and, using a wooden spoon, stir to combine. Fold in half of the reserved bacon mixture until evenly distributed through the batter.

6. Pour the remaining 3 tablespoons of the melted butter into an 8-inch square baking dish. Scrape the batter into the baking dish, slightly smoothing the top. Spoon the remaining bacon mixture over the top and place in the oven.

7. Bake for 30 minutes, or until a cake tester inserted into the center comes out clean and the top is crisp.

8. Remove the baking dish from the heat and let it rest for 10 minutes before cutting and serving.

137

Apple–Caramel Bread

MAKES 1 9-INCH LOAF

1½ cups sifted all-purpose flour

1 teaspoon ground cinnamon

½ teaspoon ground nutmeg

½ teaspoon ground cloves

½ teaspoon baking soda

¼ teaspoon baking powder

¼ teaspoon salt

1 cup light brown sugar

½ cup canola oil

2 large eggs, room temperature

1 cup unsweetened applesauce

Crumb Topping

1 cup dark brown sugar

¼ cup all-purpose flour

1 tablespoon apple pie spice mix

4 tablespoons unsalted butter, chilled and cut into pieces

1. Preheat the oven to 325°F.

2. Generously spray the interior of a 9-inch loaf pan with nonstick baking spray. Set aside.

3. Combine the flour with the cinnamon, nutmeg, cloves, baking soda, baking powder, and salt in a medium mixing bowl. Set aside.

4. Combine the brown sugar and oil in the bowl of a standing electric mixer fitted with the paddle attachment. Beat on medium until light. Add the eggs, 1 at a time, beating well to incorporate. Add the applesauce and beat to blend.

5. With the motor on low, slowly begin adding the dry ingredients, beating to incorporate. When all of the ingredients have been combined, scrape the batter into the prepared pan, lightly smoothing the top.

6. Make the topping. Combine the brown sugar, flour, and spice mix in the bowl of a food processor fitted with the metal blade attachment. Process until just combined. Add the butter and process, using quick on-and-off turns, until just crumbly.

7. Sprinkle the topping over the batter and place in the oven. Bake for 1 hour, or until a cake tester inserted into the center comes out clean and the topping is golden brown.

8. Remove the loaf pan from the oven and set it on a wire rack to cool for at least 15 minutes before cutting.

This is technically a tea bread—that is, one that can be served at tea time or breakfast with a steaming hot cup of your preferred beverage. The caramel scent comes from the combination of the dark brown sugar and butter in the topping, which can also be used for cupcakes or coffee cakes.

Apple Butter–Banana Bread

MAKES 1 9-INCH LOAF

3 very ripe bananas, peeled and mashed

½ cup Apple Butter (see page 33) *or* other fine quality apple butter

2 large eggs, beaten, room temperature

4 tablespoons unsalted butter, room temperature

2 cups all-purpose flour, sifted

⅔ cup granulated sugar

½ teaspoon baking powder

1. Preheat the oven to 325°F.

2. Generously spray the interior of a 9-inch loaf pan with nonstick baking spray. Set aside.

3. Combine the bananas and apple butter in a medium mixing bowl. Beat in the eggs and when incorporated, beat in the butter. When blended, beat in the flour, sugar, and baking powder until well incorporated.

4. Scrape the batter into the prepared pan and place in the oven.

5. Bake for 1 hour, or until a cake tester inserted into the center comes out clean and the topping is golden brown.

6. Remove the loaf pan from the oven and set it on a wire rack to cool for 10 minutes; then, invert the loaf onto the rack. Turn the loaf over and allow to cool for 45 minutes, or until completely cool before slicing.

NOTE: *All of the ingredients should be at room temperature because if they are cold, the butter will harden and not blend into the flour.*

140

Famous Fly Creek Apple–Cheddar Bread

MAKES 1 9-INCH LOAF

3 cups all-purpose flour

1½ tablespoons baking powder

1 teaspoon cayenne pepper *or* to taste

½ teaspoon baking soda

½ teaspoon salt

1 cup shredded zucchini, well drained

¾ cup shredded fine quality Cheddar cheese

⅓ cup chopped scallions

1 teaspoon freshly grated lemon zest

1 cup buttermilk

2 large eggs, room temperature

¼ cup canola oil

1. Preheat the oven to 350°F.

2. Generously coat the interior of a 9 × 5–inch loaf pan with nonstick baking spray. Set aside.

3. Place the flour, baking powder, cayenne, baking soda, and salt in a large mixing bowl, stirring to combine. Add the zucchini, cheese, scallions, and lemon zest, tossing to completely combine the ingredients. Set aside.

4. In another bowl, whisk together the buttermilk, eggs, and oil. When well-blended, pour the liquid ingredients into the zucchini mixture, stirring to just combine. The mixture should be moistened but not wet and smooth.

5. Scrape the mixture into the prepared pan. Place in the oven and bake for 1 hour, or until a cake tester inserted into the center comes out clean.

6. Remove the loaf pan from the oven and transfer to a wire rack to cool for 15 minutes before unmolding.

7. Serve warm or at room temperature. May be frozen up to 3 months.

141

Grandma Sharon Crain's Apple Bread

MAKES 2 9-INCH LOAVES

3 cups all-purpose flour, sifted

¾ teaspoon salt

¾ cup vegetable shortening

1½ cups granulated sugar

3 large eggs, room temperature

1½ teaspoons baking soda

3 tablespoons buttermilk

1½ teaspoons pure vanilla extract

3 cups peeled, diced apples

Topping

¼ cup light brown sugar

¼ cup all-purpose flour

1½ teaspoons ground cinnamon

4 tablespoons unsalted butter, room temperature

1. Preheat the oven to 325°F.

2. Lightly coat the interior of 2 9-inch loaf pans, 1 2-quart round baking dish, or 1 rectangular baking pan with nonstick baking spray. Set aside.

3. Combine the flour and salt in a small mixing bowl. Set aside.

4. Place the shortening in the bowl of a standing electric mixer fitted with the paddle attachment. Add the sugar and beat on medium until light and fluffy. Add the eggs, 1 at a time, beating well after each addition.

5. Dissolve the baking soda in the buttermilk and add to the creamed mixture, alternating with the flour mixture, beating to blend. Add the vanilla and beat until just incorporated.

6. Remove the bowl from the mixer and fold in the apples.

7. Scrape an equal portion of the batter into each of the prepared loaf pans.

8. Make the topping. Combine the sugar, flour, and cinnamon in a small mixing bowl. Add the butter and, using a pastry blender or your fingertips, blend until crumbly.

9. Sprinkle an equal portion of the topping over each loaf. Place in the oven and bake for 1 hour and 15 minutes, or until a cake tester inserted into the center comes out clean.

10. Remove the loaf pan from the oven and transfer it to a wire rack to cool for 15 minutes before cutting and serving.

142

Sharon Crain is a true part of Brenda's family and has been for as long as she can remember. Today, Grandma Sharon does the Michaels family's mending and cooks special dishes for us when we are busy at the Mill. She is always there, just like a mom or grandma. We don't know what we would do without her.

143

Fly Creek Cider Biscuits

2 cups all-purpose flour

4 teaspoons baking powder

2 teaspoons granulated sugar

½ teaspoon salt

5 tablespoons plus 1 teaspoon unsalted butter, chilled and cut into pieces

¾ cup apple cider

1 tablespoon cinnamon-sugar

1. Preheat the oven to 450°F.

2. Combine the flour, baking powder, sugar, and salt in a large mixing bowl. Add the butter and, using a pastry blender or your fingertips, work the butter into the flour until the mixture is crumbly. Slowly add the cider, stirring until a soft dough forms and the dough pulls away from the side of the bowl.

3. Using Wondra flour, lightly flour a clean work surface. Scrape the dough onto the floured surface and form into a ball. Then, pat the ball out to a circle ½ inch thick.

4. Using a floured 2½-inch round biscuit cutter, cut out the dough. Gather up the trimmings and again form them with a ½-inch thickness and continue cutting biscuits until you have used all of the dough.

5. Place the biscuits 1 inch apart on an ungreased baking sheet. Using the tines of a kitchen fork, pierce the top of each biscuit. Lightly sprinkle each one with cinnamon-sugar and place in the oven.

6. Bake for 15 minutes, or until puffed and golden brown.

7. Remove the baking sheet from the oven. Serve the biscuits hot with butter and apple butter.

These biscuits fill the house with an aroma of apple pie baking—a great way to wake up the household on a chilly morning.

Apple Rolls

3 cups peeled, diced Crispin apples

1 tablespoon fresh lemon juice

⅓ cup granulated sugar

½ teaspoon ground cinnamon

1 large egg, lightly beaten, room temperature

⅔ cup whole milk

2 cups sifted all-purpose flour, plus more for dusting

1 tablespoon baking powder

1 teaspoon salt

⅓ cup vegetable shortening

1. Preheat the oven to 400°F.

2. Lightly coat a baking sheet with nonstick vegetable spray. Set aside.

3. Combine the apples with the lemon juice in a medium mixing bowl, tossing to coat. Add the sugar and cinnamon and again toss to coat evenly. Set aside.

4. Combine the egg and milk together in a small mixing bowl, whisking to blend completely. Set aside.

5. Sift the flour, baking powder, and salt together into a medium mixing bowl. Add the shortening and, using your fingertips or a pastry blender, cut the shortening into the flour mixture until small lumps appear.

6. Remove 1 cup of the flour mixture and work it into the milk mixture. When blended, add just enough of the wet mixture to the remaining dry ingredients to make a soft dough that holds together.

7. Dust a clean, flat work surface with flour. Place the dough in the center and lightly knead until a smooth, soft dough forms. Using a rolling pin, roll the dough out to a rectangle 10 inches wide and 18 inches long.

8. Sprinkle the apple mixture over the entire surface of the dough. Roll the dough up and over the apples to make a jellyroll shape. Using a sharp knife, cut the dough, crosswise, into 1-inch slices.

9. Place the slices, cut side down, on the prepared baking sheet. Place in the oven and bake for 20 minutes, or until golden brown and slightly puffed.

10. Remove the baking sheet from the oven and serve warm or at room temperature.

Cheese Crackers

MAKES ABOUT 4 DOZEN CRACKERS

4½ cups all-purpose flour

¾ teaspoon salt

½ teaspoon baking soda

½ cup vegetable shortening, chilled

1½ cups water

Wondra flour, for dusting

We always have crackers and pretzels on hand when tasting our famous New York State Mill-aged Cheddar Cheese. These simple home-made crackers are similar to those we use and are not difficult to make. These are terrific to keep on hand to serve not only with cheese but also with soups or salads.

1. Preheat the oven to 350°F.

2. Line 2 baking sheets with silicone baking liners or parchment paper. Set aside.

3. Combine the flour, salt, and baking soda in a large mixing bowl. Add the vegetable shortening and, using your fingertips, work the shortening into the flour until the mixture is crumbly. Slowly add the water, stirring to blend.

4. Using the Wondra flour, lightly flour a clean work surface. Scrape the dough onto the floured surface and knead for 5 minutes, or until a smooth dough forms.

5. Cut the dough into 4 equal pieces.

6. Again, lightly flour the work surface with Wondra flour. Working with 1 piece of the dough at a time, roll out to a ⅛-inch thickness and then, using a 1½-inch round biscuit cutter, cut the dough into circles.

7. Carefully transfer each circle to the prepared baking sheets, leaving about an inch between each one. Using a kitchen fork or a toothpick, prick the top of each circle. If desired, you can sprinkle on flavoring here (see note).

8. When the baking sheets are full, place in the oven and bake for 18 minutes, or until set, slightly puffed, and just beginning to color.

9. Remove the baking sheets from the oven and transfer the crackers to wire racks to cool.

NOTE: *You can change the flavor by sprinkling the tops before baking with sea salt, cracked pepper, grated Parmesan cheese, rosemary needles, or almost any fresh herb you prefer.*

Desserts

Apple Pie with Caramel Sauce

MAKES 1 9-INCH PIE

1 unbaked Plain Pie Pastry (recipe follows) rolled out for a double crust pie *or* 2 refrigerated store-bought single piecrusts

2½ pounds sweet-tart apples, peeled, cored, and cut lengthwise into pieces about ¼ inch thick

1 cup granulated sugar

¼ cup all-purpose flour

1 teaspoon ground cinnamon

¼ teaspoon ground ginger

¼ teaspoon salt

2 tablespoons apple cider

2 tablespoons unsalted butter, melted

1 large egg

1 tablespoon heavy cream

1 tablespoon cinnamon-sugar

Caramel Sauce (see page 154) (optional)

1. Roll out Plain Pie Pastry for a double crust pie (or the refrigerated single piecrusts, if using). Fit one of the pastry circles into the pie pan as directed in the following recipe for Plain Pie Pastry. Set the lined pie pan aside.

2. Preheat the oven to 375°F.

3. Combine the apples, sugar, flour, cinnamon, ginger, and salt in a large mixing bowl, tossing to blend well.

4. Combine the apple cider and butter in a small mixing bowl and, when blended, pour over the apple mixture, tossing to coat.

5. Place the apples into the prepared pie pan and cover with the top crust as directed in the Plain Pie Pastry recipe that follows. Crimp the edges together.

6. Place the egg in a small mixing bowl and whisk the cream into it to make an egg wash. Using a pastry brush, lightly coat the top of the pie with the egg wash. Then, sprinkle the top with the cinnamon-sugar.

7. Place the pie in the oven and bake for 30 minutes. Turn, lower the heat to 350°F, and continue to bake for another hour, or until the top is golden brown and the apple filling is bubbling. If the crust darkens too much before the pie is completely baked, tent with aluminum foil or gently crimp aluminum foil around the edges. For easy oven cleanup, bake the pie on a nonstick baking sheet with sides.

8. Remove the pie from the oven and transfer it to a wire rack to cool for at least 1 hour before cutting and serving with the Caramel Sauce, if using.

PLAIN PIE PASTRY

MAKES ENOUGH FOR 1 9-INCH DOUBLE CRUST PIE

2½ cups all-purpose flour, sifted, plus more for dusting

¼ teaspoon salt

Pinch granulated sugar

¾ cup plus 1 tablespoon vegetable shortening, chilled

1 stick unsalted butter, cut into cubes and chilled

½ cup ice water

1 teaspoon cider vinegar

1. Combine the flour, salt, and sugar in the bowl of a food processor fitted with the metal blade attachment. Process to aerate and blend.

2. Add the shortening and butter and, using quick on-and-off turns, process until just crumbly. With the motor running, add the water and vinegar and process just until the dough begins to ball. Scrape the dough from the bowl and divide it into 2 equal pieces. Smooth each piece into a round disk, wrap each piece in plastic wrap, and refrigerate for 30 minutes to chill before rolling. (After chilling, the dough may be frozen; thaw before using.)

3. When you are ready to roll out the crust, remove 1 piece of dough from the refrigerator at a time.

4. Lightly flour a clean, flat work surface, as well as a rolling pin.

5. Unwrap the dough and place it in the center of the floured surface. Smooth the edges to keep them from breaking as you roll.

6. Using quick, short strokes and rolling from the center out, begin rolling the dough, continually moving from the center out in every direction. Lift the rolling pin gently as you near the edges to prevent breakage. Continue rolling until you have an even circle that is ½ inch thick and 2 inches wider than your pie plate. Do not overwork or handle the dough too much or it will toughen.

7. Gently lift the pastry circle by folding it in half over the rolling pin and slip it, still folded, into the pie plate. Unfold to cover the bottom of the pie plate and remove the rolling pin. Do not stretch the dough or it will shrink away from the pie plate when baked. If the pastry tears, carefully pinch it together or patch if you have any leftover dough. Smooth the pastry into the pie plate with quick pressing movements, working carefully so there are no holes.

8. If you are using the bottom crust only, press the dough firmly against the edge of the plate. Turn the excess pastry around the edge under the rim to form a thick edge. Starting at the edge opposite your body, pinch the dough between your thumb and index finger around the edge of the plate at 1-inch intervals, forming a fluted design. Keep turning the pie plate as you go. You may leave the edge fluted or flatten it slightly by pressing down lightly with the tines of a kitchen fork, taking care that the pressure on the fork is downward and toward the center of the pie. To prevent breakage and burning, make sure that the outer edge is smooth and uniform.

9. If you're making a double crust pie, proceed as for a single crust through fitting the crust into the bottom. Once the dough is firmly against the edge of the plate allow the excess dough to hang over the edge of the plate until the top crust is to be fitted on.

10. After filling the bottom crust, roll out and lift the top crust as directed above. Unfold over the filling to cover and evenly hang over the edge. Attach to the bottom crust by pressing the 2 layers of excess dough together. Fold the pressed dough edge up and inward, making a rim around the edge of the pie plate. Starting at the edge opposite your body, pinch dough between thumb and index finger around the edge of the plate at 1-inch intervals, forming a fluted design. Keep turning the pie plate as you go.

11. There are several ways to finish a double crust pie so that the internal steam escapes as the pie bakes. The easiest is to randomly pierce the unbaked top crust with the tines of a kitchen fork or to cut slashes across the top. Another is to insert a ceramic pie funnel into the center of the unbaked top crust. You can also use small decorative cutters to cut a pattern in the top crust before you place it over the filling, or you can make a lattice top by cutting the top pastry into strips and then weaving them over the top of the pie starting with the longest strips in the center.

CARAMEL SAUCE

½ cup granulated sugar

½ cup light brown sugar

¼ cup cold water

6 tablespoons unsalted butter, cut into pieces

½ cup heavy cream, room temperature

2 tablespoons hard apple cider

½ teaspoon ground cinnamon

1. Combine the granulated and brown sugars with the cold water in a heavy-bottomed saucepan over medium–high heat. Bring to a boil, stirring constantly, to dissolve the sugars. Continue to boil, frequently brushing down the edges of the pan with a wet pastry brush to keep the sugars from crystallizing, for 10 minutes, or until the mixture is a deep golden brown.

2. Lower the heat to very low and add the butter in pieces, stirring vigorously to incorporate. Work carefully as the mixture will bubble quickly. Beat in the cream, hard cider, and cinnamon, and cook for 1 or 2 minutes.

3. Remove from the heat and set aside to cool for 15 minutes.

4. Serve warm or let cool completely, place in a covered container, and refrigerate for up to 1 week. Reheat before serving.

Apple–Sour Cream Pie

MAKES 1 9-INCH PIE

1 unbaked Plain Pie Pastry (see page 152) rolled out for a double crust pie *or* 2 refrigerated store-bought single piecrusts

2½ pounds tart green apples, peeled, cored, and cut lengthwise into thick pieces

½ cup all-purpose flour

½ cup granulated sugar

1 teaspoon ground cinnamon

1 large egg, beaten, room temperature

1 cup sour cream

5 tablespoons plus 1 teaspoon unsalted butter, cut into pieces

1. Fit one of the pastry circles into the pie pan as directed in the recipe for Plain Pie Pastry on page 152. Set the lined pie pan aside.

2. Preheat the oven to 400°F.

3. Place the apples in a large mixing bowl. Add the flour, sugar, and cinnamon, tossing to evenly coat the apples.

4. Add the egg and sour cream and again toss to blend thoroughly.

5. Spoon the mixture into the bottom crust, randomly place the butter pieces over the top, and cover with the top crust as directed for a lattice top in the Plain Pie Pastry recipe on page 152. Crimp the edges together.

6. Place the pie in the oven and bake for 15 minutes. Lower the heat to 350°F and continue to bake for an additional 20 minutes, or until the crust is golden and the filling is bubbling.

7. Remove the pie from the oven and transfer it to a wire rack to cool for at least 15 minutes before cutting into wedges and serving.

Marlborough Pie

MAKES 1 9-INCH PIE

1 unbaked Plain Pie Pastry crust (see page 152) *or* 1 single refrigerated store-bought piecrust

1 cup unsweetened applesauce

4 large eggs, beaten, room temperature

1 cup granulated sugar

¼ cup fresh lemon juice

1 teaspoon freshly grated lemon zest

3 tablespoons unsalted butter, melted

1. Roll out Plain Pie Pastry for a single crust pie (or the refrigerated single piecrust, if using).

2. Fit the pastry circle into the pie pan as directed in the recipe for Plain Pie Pastry on page 152. Set the lined pie pan aside.

3. Preheat the oven to 450°F.

4. Combine the applesauce with the eggs, sugar, lemon juice, and zest in a medium mixing bowl. Using a whisk, beat to combine well. Whisk in the butter and pour into the pie shell.

5. Place the pie in the oven and bake for 15 minutes. Lower the heat to 350°F and continue to bake for an additional 20 minutes, or until the center is set.

6. Remove the pie from the oven and transfer it to a wire rack to cool.

This easy recipe is particularly good when made with homemade unsweetened applesauce, but if you don't have the time, use an excellent quality unsweetened organic applesauce.

Boiled Maple–Apple Cider Pie

MAKES 1 9-INCH PIE

4 cups apple cider

1 unbaked Plain Pie Pastry crust (see page 152) *or* 1 single refrigerated store-bought piecrust

3 large eggs, separated

1 cup pure maple syrup

¼ cup cool water

1 tablespoon unsalted butter, melted

½ teaspoon cinnamon-sugar

This pie absolutely sings with the aromas of a Central New York kitchen in the fall—apples, cider, and maple syrup. That's it!

1. Place the cider in a medium saucepan over medium–high heat and bring to a boil. Lower the heat slightly and continue to boil for 15 minutes, or until reduced to ½ cup. Remove from the heat and pour into a medium mixing bowl and set aside to cool.

2. Roll out Plain Pie Pastry for a single crust pie (or the refrigerated single piecrust, if using).

3. Fit the pastry circle into the pie pan as directed in the recipe for Plain Pie Pastry on page 152. Set the lined pie pan aside.

4. Preheat the oven to 350°F.

5. When the cider is cool, whisk in the egg yolks, syrup, water, and butter. Set aside.

6. Place the egg whites in another medium mixing bowl and, using a handheld electric mixer, beat until soft peaks form.

7. Gently fold the beaten egg whites into the cider mixture. Pour into the pie shell, sprinkle with cinnamon-sugar, and place in the oven.

8. Bake the pie for 30 minutes, or until the tip of a small sharp knife inserted into the center comes out clean.

9. Remove from the oven and transfer to a wire rack to cool for at least 30 minutes before cutting and serving.

Fly Creek Apple–Cheddar Pie

MAKES 1 9-INCH DOUBLE CRUST PIE

2½ pounds tart green apples, peeled, cored, and cut lengthwise into thick slices

2 teaspoons fresh lemon juice

¾ cup granulated sugar

2 tablespoons all-purpose flour

1 teaspoon ground cinnamon

½ teaspoon ground nutmeg

Mill-Aged Cheddar Pie Pastry (see page 37) rolled out for a double crust pie

2 tablespoons unsalted butter, cut into small pieces

¼ cup grated New York State Fly Creek Cider Mill Mill-aged Cheddar cheese *or* other fine quality Cheddar cheese

1. Preheat the oven to 400°F.

2. Place the apples and lemon juice in a large mixing bowl, tossing to blend. Add the sugar, flour, cinnamon, and nutmeg, again tossing to evenly distribute.

3. Fit one of the pastry circles into the pie pan as directed in the recipe for Mill-Aged Cheddar Pie Pastry on page 37.

4. Spoon the mixture into the bottom crust. Evenly distribute the butter over the apples. Cover with the top crust as directed on page 37. Crimp the edges together.

5. Place the pie in the oven and bake for 15 minutes. Sprinkle the top with the cheddar cheese, lower the heat to 350°F, and continue to bake for an additional 20 minutes, or until the crust is golden and the filling is bubbling.

6. Remove the pie from the oven and transfer it to a wire rack to cool for at least 15 minutes before cutting into wedges and serving.

Apple Pizza

4 medium Crispin (or heirloom tart) apples, peeled, cored, halved, and cut lengthwise into paper-thin slices

Juice of 1 lemon

3 tablespoons apple cider

½ cup granulated sugar

3 tablespoons Wondra flour

1 teaspoon ground cinnamon

1 unbaked Plain Pie Pastry crust (see page 152) *or* 1 refrigerated store-bought single piecrust

3 tablespoons unsalted butter, melted

3 tablespoons cinnamon-sugar

1. Place the apple slices in a large mixing bowl. Sprinkle with the lemon juice, add the cider, and toss to keep them from discoloring. Add the sugar, flour, and cinnamon. Toss to coat well.

2. Preheat the oven to 375°F.

3. Lightly flour a clean, flat work surface. Place the pastry in the center and, using a rolling pin, roll the dough, working from the center out, into a circle approximately 11 inches in diameter and ¼ inch thick. Carefully transfer the dough circle to a pizza pan or pizza stone.

4. Fold about ½ inch of the edge under itself all around to give the pastry circle a double thickness around the rim. Using your fingertips, crimp a neat, fluted rim of dough.

5. Working from the outside edge toward the center, make concentric circles of slightly overlapping apple slices, with the outside edge of the slices toward the outside edge of the dough. When the center is reached, drizzle the melted butter over the apples and sprinkle the entire top with cinnamon sugar.

6. Place the pizza in the oven and bake for 40 minutes, or until the apples are tender, caramelized, and beginning to brown around the edges and the crust is golden brown.

7. Remove the pizza from the oven and allow it to cool for 15 minutes before cutting. May be served warm or at room temperature.

Although not really pizza, this is a very appealing dessert for both children and adults. Take your time in placing the apples so, when baked, the top is very decorative. It is particularly delicious warm served with a scoop of ice cream.

Tarte Tatin

MAKES 1 8-INCH TART

¾ cup sugar, either granulated *or* light brown

¼ cup cold water

1 stick unsalted butter

4 large tart apples, peeled, cored, and cut into quarters

Flour, for dusting

1 piece frozen puff pastry (see sidebar)

This is an easy way to make the classic French apple tart. Try to find the best frozen puff pastry you can—those made with butter are the best.

1. Preheat the oven to 375°F.

2. Combine the sugar with the cold water in an 8-inch nonstick, ovenproof frying pan over low heat. Cook, stirring constantly, for 4 minutes, or until the sugar has dissolved. Raise the heat to medium and bring to a boil. Allow to cook, without stirring, at a gentle boil for 8 minutes, or until a golden syrup has formed. Add the butter and continue to cook, stirring until completely blended.

3. Remove the pan from the heat and carefully arrange the apples, cut sides facing up, in a slightly overlapping circle in the caramel.

4. Lightly flour a clean, flat work surface. Using a rolling pin, roll the pastry out to 10 inches around; then, cut it into a circle 9 inches in diameter. Place the pastry circle over the apples and fold the excess edge under to enclose the apples.

5. Using a paring knife, cut at least 4 slits in the center of the pastry to allow steam to escape.

6. Place the pan in the oven and bake for 35 minutes, or until the pastry has puffed and is golden brown.

7. Remove the pan from the oven and transfer it to a wire rack to rest for 5 minutes.

8. Using a small, sharp knife, loosen the edges from the pan and then carefully turn the tart out onto a serving plate. Serve warm with whipped cream, frozen vanilla or coffee yogurt, or caramel ice cream, if desired.

Brenda's Apple Upside-Down Cake

MAKES 1 10-INCH ROUND CAKE

1 cup pure maple syrup

3 tart apples, peeled, cored, and cut lengthwise into 8 equal pieces

2 cups all-purpose flour

1 teaspoon baking powder

½ teaspoon baking soda

½ teaspoon salt

¾ cup buttermilk

3 large eggs, room temperature

2 teaspoons pure vanilla extract

1½ sticks unsalted butter, room temperature

1⅓ cups granulated sugar

1. Preheat the oven to 350°F.

2. Generously coat the interior of a 10-inch round cake pan with nonstick spray. Set aside.

3. Place the maple syrup in a small saucepan over medium heat and bring to a boil. Lower the heat and cook at a bare simmer for 20 minutes, or until reduced to ¾ cup. Remove from the heat and swirl the reduced syrup over the bottom of the prepared cake pan.

4. Slightly overlap the apple slices in concentric circles over the bottom of the pan. You should have enough to make 2 complete circles.

5. Combine the flour, baking powder, baking soda, and salt in a medium mixing bowl. Set aside.

6. Combine the buttermilk with the eggs and vanilla in another medium mixing bowl, whisking to blend completely. Set aside.

7. Place the butter in the bowl of a standing electric mixer fitted with the paddle attachment. Beat on low to soften. Add the sugar, raise the speed to medium, and beat until very light and fluffy.

8. With the motor running on low, alternately add the dry ingredients and the buttermilk mixture to the butter–sugar mixture, beating to make a smooth batter.

9. Carefully pour the batter over the apples, working slowly so that you don't move the apples from their uniform circle. When all of the batter has been poured, carefully smooth the top of the cake with an offset spatula.

10. Place the cake pan in the oven and bake for 90 minutes, or until golden brown on the top, bubbling at the sides, and a cake tester inserted into the center comes out clean.

11. Remove the cake pan from the oven and set it on a wire rack to cool for 45 minutes.

12. Place a serving plate on top of the cake and invert the pan onto the plate. Carefully tap the bottom to dislodge the cake from the pan.

13. Cut the cake into wedges and serve still slightly warm with a dollop of frozen vanilla yogurt, Greek-style yogurt, or vanilla, cinnamon, or any nut-flavored ice cream.

Apple–Pumpkin Cake

MAKES 1 9-INCH BUNDT CAKE

3 cups all-purpose flour, plus more for dusting

1 teaspoon baking soda

½ teaspoon ground cinnamon

½ teaspoon ground nutmeg

½ teaspoon ground cloves

½ teaspoon ground ginger

¼ teaspoon salt

1 stick unsalted butter, room temperature, plus more for greasing

2 cups packed light brown sugar

2 large eggs, room temperature

1½ cups peeled, grated tart apples

1½ cups pumpkin purée

Juice and freshly grated zest of 1 lemon

1 teaspoon pure vanilla extract

1 cup chopped walnuts

¾ cup golden raisins

¼ cup confectioners' sugar

1. Preheat the oven to 350°F.

2. Generously butter and flour the interior of a 9-inch Bundt pan or an 11 × 7–inch rectangular baking pan. Set aside.

3. Sift the flour, baking soda, cinnamon, nutmeg, cloves, ginger, and salt together. Set aside.

4. Place the butter in the bowl of a standing electric mixer fitted with the paddle attachment and beat on low to soften. Add the brown sugar and raise the speed to medium. Beat for 4 minutes, or until light and creamy. Add the eggs and beat until just incorporated. Add the apples, pumpkin, lemon juice and zest, and vanilla, beating to blend well.

5. Add the reserved dry ingredients and beat until just incorporated.

6. Remove the bowl from the mixer and stir in the walnuts and raisins.

7. Scrape the batter into the prepared Bundt pan. Place in the oven and bake for 1 hour, or until a cake tester inserted near the center comes out clean.

8. Remove from the oven and set on a wire rack to cool for 10 minutes. Then, invert the pan onto the wire rack and tap the cake loose. Allow it to cool for another 20 minutes. Then, place the confectioners' sugar in a fine mesh sieve and tap the edge of the sieve over top of the cake to lightly dust.

9. Serve warm or at room temperature.

166

This cake keeps extremely well, stored, covered, at room temperature for up to 2 days, or refrigerated for up to 1 week.

Easy Apple Cake

MAKES 1 8-INCH SQUARE PAN

1 cup all-purpose flour

½ teaspoon ground cinnamon

½ teaspoon baking soda

½ teaspoon salt

1 stick unsalted butter, room temperature

1 cup granulated sugar

1 large egg, room temperature

1 pound tart apples, peeled, cored, and cut lengthwise into thin slices

1. Preheat the oven to 350°F.

2. Coat a nonstick 8-inch square baking pan with nonstick baking spray. Set aside.

3. Sift the flour, cinnamon, baking soda, and salt together. Set aside.

4. Place the butter in the bowl of a standing electric mixer fitted with the paddle attachment and beat on low to soften. Add the sugar and raise the speed to medium. Beat for 4 minutes, or until light and creamy. Add the egg and beat to incorporate.

5. With the motor running, slowly add the flour mixture. The batter will be very stiff.

6. Remove the bowl from the mixer and stir in the apples. When blended, scrape the batter into the prepared baking pan, using a spatula to smooth the top.

7. Place in the oven and bake for 45 minutes, or until a cake tester inserted into the center comes out clean.

8. Remove from the oven and transfer to a wire rack to cool for at least 15 minutes before cutting into squares and serving.

Apple Fritters

MAKES ABOUT 24 FRITTERS

1 cup all-purpose flour

¼ cup granulated sugar

1 teaspoon baking powder

¼ teaspoon salt

2 large eggs, room temperature, separated

½ cup whole milk

1 teaspoon unsalted butter, melted

5 Crispin apples

About 2 quarts vegetable oil, for frying

¼ cup confectioners' sugar

1. Sift the flour, granulated sugar, baking powder, and salt together into a medium mixing bowl. Set aside.

2. Place the egg whites in a small mixing bowl and, using a handheld electric mixer, beat on high until soft peaks form. Set aside.

3. Place the egg yolks in a medium mixing bowl. Still using the handheld electric mixer, beat on medium for 1 or 2 minutes to lighten. Add the milk and beat on low to blend. Add the flour mixture, beating to incorporate. When blended, add the melted butter and beat until thoroughly blended.

4. Fold the reserved egg whites into the batter, taking care to blend well.

5. Peel the apples. Using a long apple corer, line the end up with the apple core at the stem end and gently twist it all the way into the apple, making an even circle straight through the apple. Then, cut each apple crosswise into ½-inch-thick slices.

6. Place the oil for frying in a deep fat fryer, large shallow saucepan, or large deep frying pan over high heat. Bring to 365°F on an instant-read thermometer.

7. Working with 1 piece at a time, dip the apple rings into the batter, allowing excess batter to drip off, and gently drop into the hot oil. Do not overcrowd the pan. Fry, turning once, for 3 minutes, or until the coating is golden brown and crisp.

8. Using a slotted spoon, lift the fried apple rings from the hot oil and place on a double layer of paper towel to drain.

9. Continue frying until all of the rings have been fried and drained.

10. Place the confectioners' sugar in a fine mesh sieve and tap the edge of the sieve over the apple fritters to lightly coat.

11. Serve warm, as is, or with melted butter and warm maple syrup.

Apple Pandowdy

MAKES ONE 8-INCH BY 12-INCH DESSERT

¼ cup all-purpose flour

¼ teaspoon salt

¼ teaspoon ground cinnamon

Dash ground nutmeg

1 cup light brown sugar

1 cup cold water

1 teaspoon cider vinegar

2 tablespoons unsalted butter, plus more for greasing

1 teaspoon fresh lemon juice

1 teaspoon pure vanilla extract

1½ pounds tart apples, peeled, cored, and cut lengthwise into thick slices

Topping

1 cup all-purpose flour

2 teaspoons baking powder

½ teaspoon salt

3 tablespoons unsalted butter, chilled

¾ cup whole milk

1. Preheat the oven to 350°F.

2. Sift the flour, salt, cinnamon, and nutmeg in a small mixing bowl. Set aside.

3. Combine the brown sugar with the water and vinegar in a medium saucepan over medium heat. When the sugar has dissolved, whisk in the reserved flour mixture. Cook, stirring constantly, for 5 minutes, or until very thick. Whisk in the butter, lemon juice, and vanilla. When blended, remove from the heat and set aside to cool.

4. Lightly coat the interior of an 8 × 12–inch baking dish with butter. Place the apples in an even layer over the bottom of the prepared dish and set aside.

5. Place the flour, baking powder, and salt in the bowl of a food processor fitted with the metal blade attachment. Process for just a moment to blend. Add the butter and process, using quick on and off turns, until crumbs form. With the motor running, add the milk and again process using quick on-and-off turns for 1 minute, or just until a soft dough forms.

6. Pour the cooled syrup over the top of the apples, taking care that it is evenly distributed.

7. Using a teaspoon, drop the biscuit dough randomly over the top of the apples. It will not cover completely.

8. Place the baking dish in the oven and bake for 40 minutes, or until the apples are bubbling and the topping is golden brown and cooked through.

9. Remove the baking dish from the oven. Serve it hot with your favorite ice cream or drizzled with heavy cream.

Johnny Appleseed Bars

MAKES 18 BARS

1 cup sifted all-purpose flour, plus more for dusting

Unsalted butter, for greasing

1 teaspoon ground cinnamon

½ teaspoon baking soda

¼ teaspoon salt

1½ cups quick oatmeal

⅔ cup packed light brown sugar

1 large egg, room temperature

1 stick unsalted butter *or* vegetable shortening, melted

1 teaspoon pure vanilla extract

½ cup chopped toasted almonds

¾ pound apples, peeled, cored, and cut lengthwise into thin slices

2 tablespoons confectioners' sugar

1. Preheat the oven to 350°F.

2. Lightly butter and flour a 9-inch square baking pan or use a nonstick pan. Set aside.

3. Sift the flour, cinnamon, baking soda, and salt together into a medium mixing bowl. Add the oats and brown sugar, stirring to blend. Stir in the egg, melted butter, and vanilla, mixing until very smooth.

4. Place half of the dough into the prepared pan, pressing with your fingertips to evenly cover the bottom of the pan.

5. Sprinkle the almonds over the dough. Then, lay an even layer of apple slices over the almonds. Set aside.

6. Place a large sheet of wax paper out on a flat work surface. Place the remaining dough in the center and cover with another piece of wax paper. Using a rolling pin, roll the dough out to a 9-inch square.

7. Remove and discard the top piece of wax paper and invert the dough over the apples. Remove and discard the remaining piece of wax paper and, using your fingertips, press the dough around the edge of the pan to cover the apples.

8. Place the baking pan in the oven and bake for 30 minutes, or until the apples are bubbling and the crust is golden brown.

9. Remove the pan from the oven and transfer it to a wire rack to cool.

10. Place the confectioners' sugar in a fine mesh sieve and tap the edge of the sieve over the dough to lightly coat.

11. When cool, using a serrated knife, cut into 18 bars of equal size.

12. Serve, or store airtight at room temperature, for up to 3 days.

Apple–Walnut Brownies

MAKES 16 2-INCH SQUARES

1 cup all-purpose flour, plus more for dusting

½ teaspoon baking powder

¼ teaspoon salt

2 ounces unsweetened chocolate

1 stick unsalted butter, plus more for greasing

2 large eggs, room temperature

1 cup granulated sugar

1 teaspoon pure vanilla extract

1½ cups peeled, finely chopped apples

½ cup chopped walnuts

1. Preheat the oven to 350°F.

2. Lightly butter and flour an 8-inch square baking pan or use a nonstick pan. Set aside.

3. Sift the flour, baking powder, and salt together. Set aside.

4. Combine the chocolate and butter in the top half of a double boiler set over boiling water. Heat, stirring frequently, for 4 minutes, or until the chocolate and butter have melted. Remove from the heat and set aside.

5. Place the eggs in the bowl of a standing electric mixer fitted with the paddle attachment. Beat on low to loosen; then, raise the speed to medium and beat for 3 minutes, or until the mixture is a light yellow and is airy. With the motor running, gradually add the sugar. When all of the sugar has been incorporated and is dissolving, pour in the warm chocolate mixture, beating to incorporate. Beat in the vanilla.

6. Add the flour mixture and beat just until blended. Remove the bowl from the mixer and scrape off the paddle attachment. Add the apples and walnuts and stir to blend.

7. Scrape the batter into the prepared pan. Place the pan in the oven and bake for 35 minutes, or until a cake tester inserted into the center comes out clean.

8. Remove the pan from the oven and transfer it to a wire rack to cool for 30 minutes.

9. Using a serrated knife, cut the brownies into 2-inch squares.

10. Remove the brownies from the pan and serve or store, airtight at room temperature, for up to 3 days.

Apple Crumble Bars

MAKES ABOUT 48 BARS

2¼ cups all-purpose flour

½ teaspoon baking powder

½ teaspoon salt

2 sticks unsalted butter, room temperature

½ cup plus 1 tablespoon lightly packed light brown sugar (divided)

1 large egg, room temperature

1 tablespoon granulated sugar

1 teaspoon ground cinnamon

3 large Crispin apples, peeled, cored, and cut into 1-inch cubes

1. Preheat the oven to 350°F.

2. Lightly coat a 15½ × 10½ × 1–inch jelly roll pan with nonstick baking spray. Set aside.

3. Sift the flour, baking powder, and salt together into a small mixing bowl. Set aside.

4. Place the butter in the bowl of a standing electric mixer fitted with the paddle attachment. Begin beating on low to soften. Then, raise the speed to medium and beat for 3 minutes, or until light and creamy.

5. With the motor running, gradually add the ½ cup of brown sugar, beating until very light and creamy. Add the egg, beating to incorporate. When blended, slowly beat in the reserved flour mixture. When the dough is blended, remove the bowl from the mixer and scrape the paddle clean.

6. Scrape the dough into the prepared pan and, using your hands, carefully press the dough into a thin, even layer over the bottom of the pan.

7. Combine the remaining tablespoon of brown sugar with the granulated sugar and cinnamon in a small mixing bowl. Set aside.

Cinnamon Crumble Topping

1 cup all-purpose flour

⅔ cup light brown sugar

⅔ cup granulated sugar

1 tablespoon ground cinnamon

1 stick unsalted butter, chilled and cut into cubes

8. Make the crumble. Combine the flour with the brown and granulated sugars and cinnamon in a small mixing bowl. Add the butter and, using your fingertips, work the butter into the dry ingredients until coarse crumbs form.

9. Place half of the sliced apples in an even layer over the dough. Sprinkle with the lemon juice and then with cinnamon-sugar. Then, top with another layer of sliced apples. Top with an even layer of the crumble.

10. Place the pan in the oven and bake for 35 minutes, or until the crust is golden, the apples are bubbling, and the crumble is lightly browned.

11. Remove the pan from the oven and set it on a wire rack to cool.

12. When cool, using a serrated knife, cut into bars.

13. Store in a single layer, airtight, at room temperature.

NOTE: *These bars run a very close second to a classic American apple pie. However, for variety, you can try making them with ripe quince or firm pears.*

Apple–Raisin Drop Cookies

MAKES ABOUT 24 COOKIES

½ cup chopped dates

½ cup peeled, chopped apple

½ cup golden raisins

½ cup cold water

2 large eggs, room temperature

1 cup plus 1 tablespoon all-purpose flour

1 teaspoon baking soda

1 teaspoon ground cinnamon

½ teaspoon ground cloves

1. Combine the dates, apple, raisins, and water in a medium saucepan over medium heat. Bring to a boil; then, immediately lower the heat slightly and cook at a soft boil for 3 minutes.

2. Remove from the heat and set aside to cool.

3. Preheat the oven to 350°F.

4. Lightly butter 2 baking sheets or use nonstick baking sheets. Set aside.

5. When the fruit mixture has cooled, place the eggs in a small mixing bowl and whisk to blend well. Set aside.

6. Sift the flour, baking soda, cinnamon, and cloves together in a medium mixing bowl and, using a wooden spoon, beat the flour mixture into the cooled fruit. When blended, beat in the eggs. The dough will be thick.

7. Drop the dough by the tablespoonful onto the prepared baking sheets. Place in the oven and bake for 10 minutes, or until lightly browned.

8. Remove from the oven and, using a spatula, transfer the cookies to wire racks to cool.

9. Store, airtight, at room temperature for up to 3 days.

NOTE: *The dried fruits add enough sugar to these healthy cookies so you really don't need any additional sugar or artificial sweetener.*

176

Apple Pie Fudge

MAKES ABOUT 16 SQUARES

2 cups granulated sugar

1 cup light brown sugar

¾ cup apple cider

½ cup plus 2 tablespoons evaporated milk

1½ sticks unsalted butter

2 cups white chocolate baking bits

¾ cup finely diced dried apple

1 teaspoon pure vanilla extract

1 teaspoon cinnamon extract

1. Line all sides of an 8 × 8–inch baking dish with nonstick aluminum foil. To ensure that the fudge comes out easily, it is a good idea to also coat the foil with nonstick vegetable spray.

2. Combine the granulated and brown sugars in a medium, heavy-bottomed saucepan over medium heat. Add the cider and evaporated milk and stir to blend. Add the butter, raise the heat, and bring to a rolling boil. Boil, stirring constantly, for 6 minutes, or until the mixture has thickened. Do not stop stirring, as you don't want the mixture to stick to the bottom of the pan and burn.

3. Remove the pan from the heat and immediately add the white chocolate bits, stirring constantly. As the chocolate begins to melt, add the apple along with the vanilla and cinnamon extracts. Continue to stir until the chocolate has dissolved completely and the mixture has blended.

4. Pour into the prepared baking dish, cover, and refrigerate for 4 hours, or until very firm.

5. When thoroughly set, cut into small squares. Store, covered, at room temperature for up to 1 day or refrigerated for up to 1 week.

We sell thousands of pounds of fudge every season at the Fly Creek Cider Mill, and this Apple Pie Fudge is one of our customer favorites. It is a wonderful holiday candy—both to put out on the table for family and friends during holiday visits and to give as a gift.

Grandma Jane's Molasses Crinkles

MAKES ABOUT 30 CRINKLES

½ cup granulated sugar

6 tablespoons white sanding sugar

2½ cups all-purpose flour

1 tablespoon ground ginger

1 tablespoon ground cinnamon

2 teaspoons baking soda

1 teaspoon ground cloves

2 sticks unsalted butter, room temperature

1 cup dark brown sugar

⅓ cup unsulphured molasses

1 large egg, room temperature

1 teaspoon fresh lemon juice

1. Preheat the oven to 350°F.

2. Line 2 baking sheets with silicone baking liners or parchment paper. If you don't do this, butter the baking sheets.

3. Place the granulated sugar in a large shallow bowl. Set aside.

4. Place the sanding sugar in another large shallow bowl. Set aside.

5. Combine the flour, ginger, cinnamon, baking soda, and cloves in a medium mixing bowl. Set aside.

6. Place the butter in the bowl of a standing electric mixer fitted with the paddle attachment. Beat on medium to soften. Add the brown sugar and beat until light, scraping down the sides of the bowl a couple of times to ensure even creaminess. When creamy, beat in the molasses. Add the egg and lemon juice and beat to incorporate.

7. Begin adding the flour mixture, a bit at a time, and beat on low until all of the dry ingredients have been blended in. Do not over-beat, as it will dry out the dough.

8. Scoop out 1 large tablespoon of dough and roll it between your palms into a smooth ball. Roll the ball in the granulated sugar and then push 1 side into the sanding sugar.

9. Place the ball, sanding sugar–coated side up, on the prepared baking sheet.

GRANDMA JANE'S MOLASSES CRINKLES (CONTINUED)

10. Continue making cookies, setting them 2 inches apart on the baking sheets.

11. Place in the oven and bake for 10 to 12 minutes, or until just barely colored around the edges and slightly rounded in the center. Take them out at this point for soft, chewy cookies. For crisp, dry cookies bake for about 3 minutes longer. Bake a few batches to figure out exactly how much baking is required to get the desired texture.

12. Remove the baking sheets from the oven and, using a spatula, transfer the cookies to wire racks to cool.

We have been selling molasses cookies at the Mill ever since Barb, Bill's mom, started selling cookies she had made from her grandma's recipe. They were an immediate hit and have never gone out of favor. This recipe is terrific because you can decide if you want soft, chewy cookies or hard, crisp ones, depending upon the length of time you bake them.

Hard Cider Sorbet

MAKES ABOUT 5 CUPS

2 pounds tart apples, peeled, cored, and finely chopped

1 cup hard cider (divided)

1 cup granulated sugar

1 cinnamon stick

1 teaspoon freshly grated orange zest

½ cup water

½ cup fresh lemon juice

1. Combine the apples with ⅓ cup of the cider in a medium saucepan over medium heat. Bring to a boil; then, reduce the heat and simmer, stirring frequently, for 15 minutes, or until the apples have softened. Remove from the heat and set aside to cool.

2. When cool, place apple mixture in a blender and process to a smooth purée. Set aside.

3. Combine the sugar, cinnamon stick, and orange zest with water in a medium saucepan over medium heat to make sugar syrup. Bring to a boil and boil for 1 minute. Remove from the heat and stir in the lemon juice. Pour mixture into a medium heat-resistant bowl and place the bowl in a large bowl filled with ice water. Let stand until the mixture is cold.

4. Strain the sugar syrup through a fine mesh sieve into a medium bowl. Measure out 2½ cups of the apple purée and add it to the syrup. Stir in the remaining ⅔ cup of hard cider.

5. Pour the mixture into an ice cream maker and process according to manufacturer's directions.

6. Store in a covered container, frozen, for up to 2 weeks.

Drinks

Apple Cider Float

MAKES 1 FLOAT

1 large scoop vanilla ice cream

¾ cup chilled apple cider

½–¾ cup chilled ginger ale

1. Place the scoop of ice cream in a large soda glass. Pour the cider over the ice cream and then top off the glass with ginger ale.

2. Use a long iced-tea spoon to stir slightly; serve immediately with a straw.

185

Frozen Apple Slushie

MAKES 4 SLUSHIES

2 cups granulated sugar

3 cinnamon sticks

3 whole cloves

1 (1-inch) piece of fresh ginger, cut crosswise into thin slices

2 cups cold water

3 cups apple cider

1. Combine the sugar with the cinnamon sticks, cloves, and ginger in a small saucepan. Add the water and place over medium–high heat. Stirring constantly, bring to a boil. Remove from the heat and set aside to cool.

2. When cool, strain through a fine mesh sieve, discarding the solids. At this point you can store the syrup, covered and refrigerated, for up to 3 months.

3. Combine the cider with ½ cup of the syrup in a blender jar. Add chopped ice to fill the jar. Process until a slushie mixture is formed. Serve immediately.

NOTE: *You will not use all of the syrup, but since it keeps for a long period, it is good to have on hand to make slushies or to use as a syrup for almost any breakfast treat or as a moistener for layer cakes.*

186

Fly Creek Cider Mill Appletini

MAKES 1 DRINK

3 ounces chilled vodka

1 ounce chilled hard cider

Tiny drop dry vermouth

Thin slice of tart apple, for garnish (optional)

1. Place all liquid ingredients in a cocktail shaker and shake to blend. Pour into a chilled martini glass and float a thin slice of tart apple on top, if using.

NOTE: *Another great hard cider drink: equal parts hard cider and seltzer and a squeeze of lime juice, garnished with a lime wedge in a tall glass over ice.*

187

Apple–Spice Cordial

MAKES 1 QUART

2 cups granulated sugar

2 cups vodka *or* gin

6 whole cloves

3 cinnamon sticks

1 dried hot red chile

1 pound tart apples, cored, and cut into pieces

Peel of 1 orange, no pith included

1. Combine the sugar and liquor in a 6-cup nonreactive container with a tight fitting lid. Add the cloves, cinnamon sticks, and chile and stir to blend.

2. Place the apple pieces and orange peel in the bowl of a food processor fitted with the metal blade attachment. Process until finely chopped. Add the chopped mixture to the sugared liquor, stirring to blend.

3. Cover and store in a cool spot, shaking or stirring once a day for 2 weeks.

4. After 2 weeks, strain through a fine sieve, pressing to extract all of the liquid, into a clean container. Discard the solids.

5. Pour into one sterilized quart container with a tight fitting lid or into 4 sterilized 1-cup containers with tight fitting lids. Store, in a cool spot, for up to 1 year.

This very light cordial absolutely sings "holiday celebration." It looks wonderful bottled in beautiful small glass bottles, such as ones that once held fancy vinegars or body lotions.

Pip's Cup

2 quarts hard cider

1 Honeycrisp apple, cored, halved, and thinly sliced

1 orange, ends trimmed, halved, and thinly sliced

1 pear, cored, halved, and thinly sliced

2–3 cups frozen green seedless grapes

1 quart ginger ale *or* ginger beer, chilled

Fresh mint leaves, for garnish

1. Pour the cider into a nonreactive container. Add the apple, orange, and pear. Cover and set aside to macerate at room temperature for 5 hours.

2. Strain the liquid through a fine mesh sieve into a clean container, discarding the solids. Cover and refrigerate for 3 hours, or until chilled.

3. When ready to serve, fill large glasses with a mixture of ice and the frozen grapes. Pour the chilled flavored cider to fill the glass about ¾ full. Top with the ginger ale or ginger beer, garnish with a mint leaf, and serve.

Hot Mulled Cider

SERVES A CROWD

4 quarts apple cider

½ cup dark brown sugar

2 teaspoons whole cloves

1 orange

1 large lemon

3 cinnamon sticks

1 (2-inch) knob fresh ginger

1 teaspoon cardamom seeds

½ teaspoon black peppercorns

1. Place the cider in a large nonreactive saucepan. Stir in the brown sugar.

2. Randomly poke the whole cloves into the orange and lemon. When studded, place the citrus in the cider.

3. Combine the cinnamon sticks, ginger, cardamom, and peppercorns in a cheesecloth bag, tying to close securely. Add the bag to the cider.

4. Place the cider over high heat and bring to a boil. Immediately lower the heat and simmer for 15 minutes.

5. Remove from the heat and allow to sit for 15 minutes in order to allow the spices to infuse the cider.

6. Pour the cider into warm mugs and serve. If desired, add a tablespoon or so of hard cider or apple brandy into each mug just before serving.

Mulled cider is one of our favorite warming drinks throughout the cold, snowy Upstate New York winter, particularly after a day of outdoor sports. If it becomes your family favorite, don't hesitate to make it in a large batch—you can bottle and refrigerate it for up to a month, and it can be warmed when needed.

ACKNOWLEDGMENTS

WE'D LIKE TO THANK the following people for their help and support in our lives and our livelihood:

Barbara and Charlie Michaels, the founders of the Fly Creek Cider Mill and Bill's wonderful parents. We thank them for having the foresight to see the great potential in the Mill.

Bill's sister, Francine, and her family, who pop in to help when called.

Grandpa Hi and Grandma Jane Michaels, who first taught Bill his hospitality and retail skills. Grandpa Hi provided great examples for Bill, as he was a fourth generation retailer in Cooperstown, New York, where Bill grew up.

Mary Wright, Bill's mentor at the hospitality school of Rochester Institute of Technology.

The late Ma and Pa Palmer (Joyce & Dwight)who showered Brenda with unconditional love to thrive anywhere and create anything. Joyce lit up a room with her smile and laughter, and Dwight could fix most anything. Together they showed their family how to live simply, and be happy, generous, and smell the roses along the way. They are greatly missed but the memories are plenty.

Sharon Crain, a true member of the Palmer family—always has been, and continues to be. When Brenda was growing up in Smyrna, New York (population 250), Sharon helped Brenda's mom raise all of the children as she has helped us raise ours. She taught us our love of great food among so many other things. We don't know what we'd do without her.

Our many friends from Smyrna, New York: We thank them for always being so supportive of the Mill.

Brenda's brother, Charlie Palmer, whose patience, kindness, loyalty, wisdom, and love has guided Brenda throughout the years; and his wife, Lisa, who shared many inspired meals in their restaurants.

Thanks to all of Brenda's other brothers, the late David Palmer, Leslie Palmer, Richard (Spike) Lamoreaux, and Neil Palmer, who helped build her strong character.

Brenda's Grandmother, Nannie Marguerite Palmer, who always cooked for everyone and was known for arriving with a basket of her fabulous cream puffs.

Genevieve Smith (Grandma Gen), who was always there for Brenda.

Judith Choate, whose expertise helped us create the cookbook we envisioned, and Steve Pool, whose photography shows all of our recipes as the mouthwatering dishes they are.

INDEX

Note: Italic page numbers indicate photos.

ABOUT THE AUTHORS

Brenda and Bill Michaels are the co-owners of the Fly Creek Cider Mill and Orchard, which they have been running since 1999. Both Brenda and Bill have won numerous entrepreneur and small business awards. They live in Cooperstown, NY.

From left to right: Henry, Brenda, Sadie, Bill, Charlie, and Barbara Michaels.

MANY OF THE RECIPES in this book are based on products made for and sold at the **Fly Creek Cider Mill and Orchard's Mill Store Marketplace**, a destination for lovers of everything food. Addressing the needs and tastes of our visitors is paramount to keeping the Mill alive for future generations to enjoy. At the Mill Store Marketplace, you can taste and purchase a variety of specialty food. Because we partner with **New York State's Pride of New York program**, many of our items are locally grown and produced. Stop by and try favorites, such as

- our famous New York State Mill-aged Cheddar cheese,
- pure maple syrup from Westford,
- fresh cheese curds from Palatine Bridge,
- honey from our local beekeepers,
- cake mixes from Rochester, and
- wines from the Finger Lakes.

You can also visit the Mill's on-line store to purchase Fly Creek Cider Mill and Orchard–branded products and other bestselling farm-to-table items. We ship mostly nonperishable, nonalcohol products with full case discounts given.

To order, visit www.flycreekcidermill.com or call the Mill during regular business hours at 607-547-9692.